VICTORIA MATTHEWSON is a hand embroidery artist specializing in needlepainting. By combining her love of nature and craft she has developed a distinctive style of embroidery using silk floss thread, creating realistic artwork inspired by British flora and fauna, with a special focus on insects.

She is proud to have built a reputation as one of the top needlepainting artists in the UK; in March 2018 she won Needlecrafter of the Year at the National Needlecraft Awards in collaboration with DMC thread. She is a member of the Society for Embroidered Work and has also created projects for *Stitch* magazine.

Visit her website at:
www.victoriamatthewson.com

Needlepainted Plants
and Pollinators

First published in 2022

Search Press Limited
Wellwood, North Farm Road,
Tunbridge Wells, Kent TN2 3DR
Great Britain

ISBN: 978-1-78221-860-9
ebook ISBN: 978-1-78126-823-0

The Publishers and author can accept no
responsibility for any consequences arising
from the information, advice or instructions
given in this publication.

SUPPLIERS

If you have any difficulty obtaining any
of the materials or equipment mentioned
in this book, then please visit the Search
Press website for details of suppliers:
www.searchpress.com

Needlepainted Plants and Pollinators

AN INSECT LOVER'S GUIDE TO SILK SHADING EMBROIDERY

VICTORIA MATTHEWSON

SEARCH PRESS

DEDICATION

For my parents.

ACKNOWLEDGEMENTS

Firstly, I must thank my husband, David, and my two girls, Evelyn and Isabella, for their patience and understanding while I worked on this book. Also for waiting for me on walks while I photographed 'interesting' insects.

I must also thank my parents who have always been unwavering in their support and love. You have always believed I can.

My heartfelt thanks go to my editor, Becky Robbins, and the team at Search Press for giving me this opportunity and believing that pollinators are worthy of their own book. Thank you for giving me the freedom to create projects that truly reflect my work and passion.

While putting this book together I have relied on so many wonderful organizations and people who inspire and educate. Thank you to Peter Coffey for putting the pollinator question in my mind in the first place and for being my sounding board for ideas and information – your photos are truly inspirational. I must also thank Paul Hetherington of the charity Buglife, who very kindly fact-checked all my insect information for each project. Buglife is a wonderful UK-based charity that aims to 'Save the small things that run the planet'. If you are inspired by anything in this book you may like to visit their website: www.buglife.org.uk

I am very lucky to live in a small Welsh village that proudly boasts Gwent Wildlife Trust's flagship nature reserve, Magor Marsh. This site has been an endless source of inspiration and my regular walks have been a comfort to me for a long time, especially this year, what with one thing and another. The commitment of all the staff and volunteers in protecting and caring for this site is inspirational – thank you so much. If you would like to learn more, visit: www.gwentwildlife.org

Finally, thank you to all of the people and organisations who are dedicated to being a voice for the little things that need our help, but are having trouble being heard.

'From far and near they come – hive bees, humble bees, and all the lesser-known bee species from wood and hedgerow bank – while moths flutter their soft wings about the summer rusty spikes, and flies come shrilling up to claim their share of the feast.'

Flora Thompson, *The Peverel Papers* (c. 1921–1927)

contents

Foreword by Iolo Williams 6

Introduction 8

All about pollinators 10

You will need 12

Transferring the design 20

Framing up 21

Stretching and mounting 22

Presentation of your embroidery 24

Inspiration 26

Planning a design 28

Needlepainting 31

Additional stitches 36

Small stitched elements 41

THE PROJECTS 44

Dog Rose and Greenbottle Fly 46

Lords-and-Ladies and Owl Midges 56

Ox-eye Daisy and Hoverfly 64

Fennel and Seven-spot Ladybird 72

Meadow Buttercup and Thick-legged Flower Beetle 80

Bramble and Gatekeeper Butterfly 90

Common Knapweed and Six-spot Burnet Moth 100

Blackthorn and Buff-tailed Bumblebee 110

Gooseberry and Common Wasp 120

My previous work 130

Templates 136

foreword by Iolo Williams

Welsh Naturalist, TV Wildlife Presenter, Conservationist and Writer

When I was asked to provide a foreword for a book on embroidery, I immediately thought that either the publisher had dialled the wrong number or my friends had devised yet another devious way to set me up. After all, I am about as talented with a needle and thread as I am with the controls of a Boeing 747, but having looked through this book and admired how Victoria takes her inspiration from nature, I felt far more comfortable penning a few words.

Make no mistake, there will be no comments on needlecraft or silk-cotton blend, but I am incredibly impressed not only by the embroidery skills and teachings on show, but also because of the way often overlooked species are used to illustrate the various techniques. As Victoria mentions in her introduction, she is extremely fortunate to have Gwent Wildlife Trust's flagship reserve, Magor Marsh, on her doorstep. Situated on the edge of the Gwent Levels, this wonderful wildlife oasis is home to kingfisher, otter, little egret and barn owl but for her subjects, the author looks to the insects, the smaller, less well-known species such as the stunning six-spot burnet moth, the pollen-laden buff-tailed bumblebee and the wonderfully named thick-legged flower beetle.

Our insects, and in particular our pollinators, are suffering catastrophic declines due mainly to a combination of habitat loss and the over-use of harmful chemicals such as pesticides and insecticides. This is touched upon here, as are some of the simple steps that can be taken to halt and reverse these declines. Simple steps they may be, but if all of us took note and acted upon them, it would make a significant difference.

The book is liberally sprinkled with plenty of stunning wildlife photographs to encourage readers to take up embroidery and to take note of the wildlife around them, and I think this is the great value of this book for someone like me who has never lifted a needle in anger. It encourages you to look closer at the wildlife around you, to become a child again and get down on your hands and knees to study its shape and colour and, above all, to appreciate it for its beauty.

After enduring one of the most difficult periods in several generations, we could all do with a hobby that combines physical exercise with mental stimulation and relaxation. The combination of wildlife and embroidery in this book delivers in droves.

introduction

In times of trouble and stress I turn to two things to calm and
focus my mind: embroidery and nature.

The benefits of both nature and embroidery to mental wellbeing
are well documented – the gentle, rhythmic movement of the
needle is meditative and soothing, while walking in nature is
proven to reduce blood pressure. But at the time of writing this
book, the world is especially troubled, and it is difficult not to feel
overwhelmed by the onslaught of warnings and bad news. Whilst
it is important to be aware of current situations and not ignore
the world, taking time to stop and focus on the small things can
be a tonic. Instead of feeling you need to save the whole world,
look closer to home, explore your garden or local park, listen
to the sounds that surround you, see what life there is when
you take time to stop. You don't need to be able to identify
every birdsong or know the name of every insect – your
interest can be instinctive rather than intellectual. If you
are inspired by what you discover you can explore it further
in a creative way. For me this is through embroidery, but it
could be through anything from gardening or photography to
painting. Or you may just want to carry on observing. Either way,
observing leads to awareness and understanding, and this can lead
to respect, which can result in change. By looking after the small
gifts nature has provided we can help the entire planet.

Like many people, I started my embroidery journey by learning
cross-stitch at primary school. We had been asked to create a basic
design and, while most children preferred to stitch square dogs
and square houses, my desire for detail was already making
itself known; I came back with a floral wreath surrounded by
a Celtic border. During my time in higher education I decided
to embroider a dress I was sewing for my graduation. I had no
training and didn't really understand different techniques, but
I started stitching flowers and butterflies in an instinctive way.
Without knowing it, I was needlepainting, but it would be another
fifteen years before I knew that this style of embroidery had a
name. When I say that it has a name, I should really say that it
has several: threadpainting, silk shading, long-and-short stitch
and (my favourite) needlepainting. Whichever term you
prefer, the general theory is the same. It is the principle
of creating embroidery that has the appearance of a
painting – literally painting with your needle and thread.

Since stitching my graduation dress, I have studied many
books about needlepainting and been inspired by the works
of other amazing artists. I have learnt the techniques that can help
to improve my work and the tools that are best suited to each
individual piece. However, the basic desire to stitch the images
that inspire me remains the same as it was back then. This is
why I love needlepainting; every artist (and I say artist as I truly
believe this is art) has their own style – there is no right or
wrong way to work.

Why insects?

Our insect populations are in trouble. At the time of writing, more than 40 per cent of insect species are in decline and the rate of extinction is eight times faster than for any animal, bird or reptile. Insects are the most varied and abundant creatures on this planet and their decline is threatening a catastrophic collapse of our natural eco-system. So why is it so difficult to get people to care? Individual species under threat of extinction can spark a great rallying cry, especially if the animal is impressive or cute, but an entire group of essential creatures is in danger and you can still buy poison at your local supermarket or garden centre to kill them. Perhaps it is because certain insects are considered pests, or that their appearance is alien to human eyes. But each insect has its place and purpose in a healthy eco-system.

If we are going to help insect numbers we need to change people's perception of these mighty little creatures; we need to foster a respect for them even if we cannot encourage love. I was once told that if you want to understand an insect you should draw it, as the skill needed to correctly represent your subject makes you study it in a methodical and intricate way. But the patience and time needed to embroider an insect, especially using a needlepainting technique, can foster a respect and love for that creature unlike any other craft. You create a bond with it as you sew, spending hour after hour considering each part of its body and its purpose, how it fits in and how it has evolved to perfectly suit its environment.

While insects are essential in many ways, from aiding decomposition to providing food for our native wildlife, perhaps the most relatable benefit is their role in pollination. Without pollinating insects our diet would be greatly reduced, our gardens would struggle, and natural habitats would seem sparse and dull without the wonderful variety of wildflowers. I had always been aware of the role that bees played in pollination, but it was a post on social media by American entomologist, Peter Coffey, that got me thinking. Below a photo of a fly on a flower it simply said 'there are more pollinators than just bees'. What insects, other than honeybees, are considered pollinators? Plants and insects have evolved alongside each other for millions of years, developing a mutually beneficial relationship that ensures the future of both – take away one and the other will suffer. When you start to understand the different ways in which plants attract pollinators you will find it fascinating, from complex trap-and-release systems to colour and scent variations. The projects in this book are aimed at celebrating these symbiotic relationships, and fostering a greater understanding and respect for plants and pollinators and the relationships that have evolved between them.

It is worth noting that I am not an entomologist. My understanding has come from basic research, a desire to learn and conversations with people far more qualified than myself. I have tried to keep the information and subject matter in this book accessible. All the insects and plants that I have focused on can be found in the United Kingdom (and many can be found in different countries worldwide) and the information given includes basic facts, history and folklore. If you are inspired by anything in this book, I would encourage you to head outside – you don't even have to leave your garden – and start marvelling and finding inspiration in the miniature world that surrounds us. And remember, it's not just bees.

all about pollinators

It has been said that if insects were to disappear overnight, the world's eco-system would collapse. And with every third mouthful of food we eat dependant on pollinators, it is easy to see how human life would be dramatically affected. Yet our understanding of the importance of insects, specifically pollinators, is woefully lacking. Recently, bees have undergone a remarkable publicity campaign, with everything from T-shirts to shopping bags emblazoned with the words 'Save the Bees'. While this campaign is certainly to be applauded, it would be wonderful to foster a more inclusive love and understanding of the role other insects play in bringing food to our table and filling our gardens and waysides with wildflowers.

If you think of pollination, most likely you automatically picture honeybees. It is true that honeybees are prolific pollinators and are responsible for somewhere between 15 and 30 per cent of insect-pollinated crops. However, the remaining 70–85 per cent are dependent on other pollinating insects such as moths, butterflies, beetles, hoverflies, wasps and 250 species of wild bees, including bumblebees. In the UK, £690 million worth of crops are pollinated each year for free by these busy insects, so consider this on a global scale! It is perhaps time that we re-assess our relationship with all pollinators, not just the ones that give us honey.

Pollinators, and indeed all insects, are sadly facing a dramatic decline in numbers. In the UK, half of our bumblebee species are declining, with three species already extinct; a third of our wild bees and hoverflies are gradually disappearing; the number of moths has decreased by a third since the 1960s; and over 70 per cent of our butterflies are in decline. This pattern is being replicated across the globe. It is difficult to imagine a world without such things as strawberries, cherries, peanuts, cotton and chocolate to name but a few, but this could become reality if we don't address the decline of our insect populations.

So why are insect numbers declining so rapidly? This cannot be pinned down to just one problem – there are many factors to consider. Intensive farming has eaten into our flower-rich habitats and urban growth has reduced areas of surrounding countryside. With 97 per cent of UK wildflower meadows lost since the 1930s it is easy to see why the loss of this incredibly important habitat would be affecting insect numbers. The increased use of pesticides has also had an impact – chemicals that were intended to harm insects considered 'pests' are also harming the very pollinators many crops rely on. Climate change should also be included, as unpredictable and extreme weather can have a dramatic effect on insect numbers as they struggle to adapt to evermore erratic conditions. If our response to this decline is purely focused on honeybees, we may never address the wider problem and insect populations may continue to fall, causing an imbalance in our eco-system and a knock-on effect on the food chain.

Encouraging insects into your garden

So how can we help? With an incredible 16 million gardens in the UK alone, think of the impact we could make to insect numbers if every gardener could commit to making small changes in the way they care for their land. Even if you don't have a garden there are ways in which you can help: if you have a windowbox or hanging basket you can still plant with insects in mind. When we think of wildlife gardens we might imagine a rather messy, overgrown environment with wildflower meadows, or bramble patches tangling over fences, but if that doesn't appeal to you there are still small changes that can help.

WHAT TO PLANT

When choosing plants for your garden, try to find nectar- and pollen-rich flowers. Plants will often be labelled as 'Perfect for Pollinators', and garden-centre staff will be happy to advise. Pollinators often prefer single- rather than double-flowered plants, and native flowers will suit your local insect population perfectly. Why not help insects and benefit from their services at the same time? Herbs, fruit trees and many vegetables are loved by pollinators and will provide you with homegrown produce. Try to consider the different seasons when planting: early pollinators will benefit from flowers such as foxgloves, cowslips and crab-apple blossom, while insects that appear later in the year appreciate cyclamen, ivy or autumn-flowering witch hazel.

USING PESTICIDES

Where possible, try to reduce your use of pesticides. While they may destroy the insects that are considered pests, they will also harm beneficial insects and wildlife. If you do need to use a pesticide, try to use it sparingly and away from known pollinators. If you can attract natural predators, infestations should become more manageable in time as a natural balance is struck.

PROVIDE A BUG HOTEL

Bug hotels can be created in a variety of ways, from large multi-storey luxury hotels made from wooden pallets and filled with everything from logs and straw to bricks, to small guest houses made from bamboo canes and a lemonade bottle. Solitary bees such as leaf cutters can be a joy to watch in the summer as they busily fill the canes with carefully nibbled leaves (see image, top left).

LEAVE YOUR LAWN

If you are happy to leave an area of your garden to grow wild, insects will love it, as it is similar to their natural environment. Leaving just a small area of lawn uncut and allowing the clover, buttercups and self-heal to grow will provide a valuable source of nectar and pollen (see image, below left).

CREATE A MINI MEADOW

If you can, set aside a small, sunny area of your garden to create a mini meadow – it will produce a splash of colour in the summer that insects will love. Check that any wildflower seeds you buy are native to where you live; in the UK this might include plants such as knapweed, red clover, bird's foot trefoil and cowslips. Sow seeds in autumn or early spring on bare soil, gently press them in and lightly water them. You will need to cut your meadow in autumn, once the seeds have dropped, and remove the cuttings.

you will need

Fabrics

Once you are familiar with needlepainting there is a wide range of fabrics that you can experiment with; when you are just starting out it is easiest to work with a tightly woven fabric such as cotton, linen or silk. I would also recommend choosing a plain fabric at first, as patterns can be quite distracting and may become distorted as you sew. I prefer to use white or undyed cotton or silk as this helps me to focus on my design and stitching. Whichever fabric you decide to use, it is advisable to wash it first to make sure it is pre-shrunk. When cutting, always cut on the grain; if you cut on the bias, the fabric may stretch and distort when framing up.

BACKING FABRIC

Needlepainting creates quite dense stitching and can be rather intensive for thin fabric, therefore a backing material is often used. A plain white cotton or calico is ideal to back and strengthen a thin top fabric and will take some of the strain when it is stretched over a frame. An old white cotton sheet can be used as backing fabric or calico is readily available and inexpensive. Calico (4) is an unbleached cotton that has not been fully processed so it can sometimes contain small pieces of husk – this will not damage your embroidery but I have found that some of the larger pieces can show through your top fabric, so check this before you start stitching.

COTTON (3)

Cotton is a natural fabric made from the cotton plant. It is a strong, inexpensive material and perfect for starting your embroidery journey. A medium-weight, tightly woven cotton that doesn't stretch is best and, as with the backing fabric, if you are just starting out and want to practise, an old sheet or pillowcase can be used to great effect.

SILK (1)

If you are using silk floss thread you may find that silk fabric is the perfect partner for your work. It is naturally very strong and has a beautiful texture and subtle shine that traditionally complements needlepainting. Silk comes in many different weights, colours and textures; dupion is a good choice for needlepainting as it has a tight weave and is stronger than other silks. Silk fibres are obtained by soaking the cocoons of the silkworm in hot water. The filament is then gradually unwound and can measure anything up to a mile long. When two silkworms spin cocoons together this can cause a slub in the fibre and this can often be seen in silk dupion. If the slubs are large it is best to avoid them in the area that you are going to be stitching, but if they are small they shouldn't cause too much of a problem, and they could even add interesting texture to your work. There are ethical reasons why some people may choose not to use silk, as it is derived from the silkworm, but there are many alternatives and plenty of information available if you would like to research the issue further for yourself.

SILK-COTTON BLEND (2)

Although I do love using silk dupion I have recently started using a white silk-cotton blend fabric. This is not always easy to obtain but if you find a good supplier it is worth trying. The weave is nice and tight, it has less shine than pure silk and the cotton makes it incredibly strong. It can also be dyed and drawn on as your design requires.

LINEN (5)

A tightly woven linen can really complement your needlepainting. Made from the fibres of the flax plant, linen is a strong, durable fabric that is coarser than silk. Linen can be dyed many colours, but a natural undyed fabric is a great starting point. Dress linen is suitable for embroidery with cotton thread and is often strong enough that you will not need a backing fabric. There are some drawbacks to using linen: it can be more expensive than cotton as it has a very labour-intensive manufacturing process and it can also crease very easily. If the fabric is continuously folded in the same place, the fibres can be damaged and the material will become unusable in that area.

Threads

The most common question I am asked about my embroidery is 'what thread do you use?' There are many different types of thread available and each will give a different result. Thick threads like crewel wool can be a good starting point as the texture can be quite forgiving, however intricate detail may be difficult. I started my needlepainting journey with cotton floss/thread and moved to silk floss/thread as it gave me greater control over the finer details in my designs and a higher sheen. Whichever thread you choose I would recommend buying enough for your whole project to ensure colour consistency – different dye batches can vary ever so slightly, which can be frustrating if you run out halfway through. You should also make sure that you store your threads away from direct sunlight as this can fade the colour. I keep mine in labelled plastic storage boxes and if I have several threads out on a rack for a specific project I will cover them with a cloth to avoid discolouration and dust.

COTTON FLOSS/THREAD

Cotton is an excellent floss to start with as it is readily available and comes in a wide variety of colours. There are threads to suit all budgets, although you may find that the packs that seemed an excellent bargain on the internet lack shine and durability. DMC and Anchor are the most widely available cotton threads – they are colourfast and have a high sheen – but there are many other brands that can be found in your local craft shop. If you are lucky enough to have a supplier nearby, why not treat yourself and pop in? There is something so exciting about browsing the multitude of colours, exploring the possibilities and getting ideas.

Skeins of stranded cotton are usually comprised of four or six threads, which can be separated according to the thickness needed for your project. Needlepainting usually requires only one thread at a time but you can mix two strands of different colours within your needle to create a shaded effect. To separate one thread from the skein, pull out a length of cotton no longer than from your thumb to your elbow, separate out a single strand and pull it vertically upwards – this will ensure that the rest of the strands do not tangle. While it is tempting to cut a much longer length of cotton it is unadvisable, as longer threads are more likely to tangle as you sew. The projects in this book can be stitched in cotton thread but some of the smaller details may be hard to achieve unless you enlarge the template slightly.

SILK FLOSS/THREAD

Silk is the most traditional thread used in needlepainting (which is why the technique is sometimes referred to as silk shading). It has a wonderful shine and, after some practice, can be very enjoyable to work with. I like to use silk floss, which is very thin thread that has not had the fibres twisted. The fibres can be split down for even finer detail, but this can make them very difficult to work with. Silk floss is not as readily available as cotton thread and may have to be purchased from specialist online suppliers; this can make colour identification difficult, so I would recommend buying a shade card if it is available. I use two main suppliers of floss silk in the UK, Pipers Silks and DeVere Yarns. Both offer excellent-quality thread and are more than happy to advise if you have any queries.

Stitching with floss silk can take some getting used to – it takes much longer than stitching with cotton, and any dry skin on your hands can cause the thread to fray. Try to keep your hands clean and moisturised but not too oily. I have stitched the projects in this book with silk floss as it is my favourite thread to work with.

In the embroidery hoop shown right, note the different finishes created using cotton (on the left) and silk threads (on the right), when embroidering the same shape and tones.

Tools

NEEDLES

There is a wide range of needles available and the choice can sometimes be baffling. Start by thinking about the type of floss you will be using and the weave of the fabric. Embroidery needles have a sharp point and a long eye to make them easier to thread. All needles come in different sizes and the larger the number, the finer the needle. If you are working with one or two strands of cotton thread a size 10 would be appropriate, but if you are using silk floss on a tightly woven fabric a size 12 embroidery needle would be more suitable. I would not recommend using anything larger than a size 9 needle for needlepainting. The needle should make a hole in the fabric through which the floss can pass – if you can hear the thread being pulled through the material then your needle is too small, but if you are left with large holes in the fabric then your needle is too big.

Needles are inexpensive and readily available to buy; however, it can be hard to find size 12 in your local craft shop, so you may need to search online. When I started, I used standard embroidery needles in sizes 10 to 12. As I progressed, I invested in handmade Japanese needles. These are very hard-wearing with an excellent point and worth the investment if needlepainting is going to be a long-term hobby. If your needle becomes blunt and does not pass easily through the fabric it should be changed for a new one.

Sharps and curved needles are useful to keep handy for lacing up your embroidery and other stitching.

PINS

Strong dressmakers' pins are useful if you are mounting your embroidery, as they will hold your fabric in position over the board while you lace the back (see page 23). They can also be used when stretching your fabric on a slate frame.

SCISSORS

A good pair of fabric scissors is essential in any sewing kit but everyone else in your house needs to be made aware that they are for cutting fabric only – using them to cut paper or toenails will blunt them! Within your embroidery kit, large fabric scissors are useful for cutting your project fabric, but they will be far too cumbersome for snipping delicate embroidery thread. A small pair of sharp scissors with a fine point will ensure your thread is left with a neat edge, making it easier to thread. Specialist embroidery scissors are available – the stork design being the most recognizable – but any small, sharp-pointed scissors will work. Again, these scissors should be used for thread only, as cutting fabric or paper will blunt them.

THIMBLE

Whether you wear a thimble while stitching or not is a personal choice, but it is useful to have one handy if your stitching becomes dense. If you are using a size 12 needle and stitching a dense area of embroidery you may find that your finger gives way to the eye of the needle before the fabric does the point, leaving a rather painful hole. Thimbles come in a variety of sizes and can be made from metal, plastic or leather. Whichever type you choose, it should fit snugly so that it does not slip off while stitching.

FABRIC PENS

The two main types of fabric pen available are water-soluble and air-soluble. Their purpose is to create a temporary drawing on your material, which will either disappear over time or can be washed out when you have finished stitching. These pens can be very useful on short-term projects, however, there are some drawbacks. If you work in an environment that can become damp, a water-soluble pen will disappear quickly (I often work in my summerhouse and have found that a carefully drawn template can disappear overnight). I have also found that these pens can leave permanent marks on some dyed fabrics, so I would recommend testing them on a spare piece of fabric before use.

STATIONERY

It is always handy to have stationery items available while you are working. When you are creating your design it is helpful to have various pens and pencils, both coloured and graphite, an eraser, a pencil sharpener and other items you might find in a school pencil case (I have found a maths set useful, with a compass, protractor and different rulers). If you are mounting your own work, a craft knife, metal ruler and cutting mat will allow you to cut your board neatly without risking damage to the surface underneath. I also like to keep a pen and paper handy for making notes as I work, perhaps to note floss colours I have used or an idea I have had for dinner that evening... either way it can be very useful!

ORT JAR

An ort jar is one of those wonderful items that serves no real purpose. It is, to put it simply, a jam jar that you put your snippets of thread in rather than dropping them on the floor or the furniture. Although I am not sure why we all feel the need to keep these snippets, there is something very satisfying about seeing the jar slowly fill – the layers of colour created by each project are rather like a soil sample showing the history of the land.

It has been suggested in the past that threads can be put out in the spring for nesting birds, but this is not recommended – any type of yarn or hair can become tangled around birds' legs or necks, causing injury and even death.

Stands

To allow both of your hands to be free for stitching you may wish to use a stand to hold your work. There are several different types of stand available and the type you choose will depend on your workspace and personal preference.

A seat frame (2) does not take up much space and allows you to work closely with your embroidery. The base plate of the frame is tucked under your thighs to hold it steady and the height is then adjusted to your preference. Seat frames will usually have a removable dowel which will either have a hoop already attached or a clamp to hold a separate frame.

If you are working at a desk you might like to use a table clamp (1). This works in a similar way to a seat frame but has an adjustable screw to allow you to clamp it on to the edge of a table instead of sitting on a base plate.

If you have the space in your work area you may like to invest in a floor stand. These can be made of metal or wood and provide a more permanent stand for your work. Floor stands often have many adjustable parts so are more adaptable to your style of working, and they have a clamp that can hold a variety of different frames and sizes of work.

Lamps

If you are blessed with perfect vision, a large window and sunny weather you may never need to use a lamp while you work. However, many people like to sew in the evening and artificial light can distort colour and strain the eye. Craft shops sell a variety of different lamps with daylight bulbs that will give you a better idea of the colours you are using and allow you to see your stitches more clearly. Needlepainting often uses tiny stitches and very fine thread so working in dim light can prove impossible.

I use a floor standing magnifying lamp, which lights the work perfectly and allows for a much closer view of the stitching. Often lamps will be adjustable to allow them to be either floor standing, used on a desk or clamped to a table. Bear in mind that magnifying your work can also magnify errors that don't look as bad when viewed normally, so don't forget to stand back and look at your work every now and then. You should always cover your magnifying lamp when not working as it could be a fire risk if the sun shines directly onto it.

Frames

Stitching any kind of embroidery without a frame can be tricky, as the fabric will wrinkle and pucker as the stitches are pulled tight, and dirt can transfer from your hands, making the final work appear dull. To avoid this it is recommended that you use one of the many types of embroidery frames that are available. This will allow you to keep your fabric tight and, if used with a stand, your hands free to work on the stitching.

HOOPS

Wooden hoops are probably the most-used frame for embroidery and are available in many different sizes at an affordable price. They are excellent for smaller projects that will not be in the hoop for too long. You should try to use a hoop that fits your entire design to avoid having to re-adjust it over work already sewn. Before hooping up your work it is advisable to wind open bias binding or a strip of cotton fabric around your bottom hoop, adding a couple of stitches to hold it in place.

It has become popular to display embroidery in the hoop, using it as a frame. A simple running stitch can be used to draw the excess fabric in around the reverse of the work. Leaving your embroidery in the hoop also gives you the opportunity of seeing the reverse, sometimes called the 'Hoop Butt' for fun. While some people might shudder at the thought of a thread-tangled reverse being seen, it can be a fascinating insight into the mechanics behind the embroidery and can be as aesthetically pleasing as the front.

INTERLOCKING BAR FRAMES

Bar frames are my favourite as they can hold the tension of your fabric over a long period of time, which is essential for larger, long-term projects. They are also light and portable and can be clipped easily into a seat frame or floor clamp.

The interlocking bars can be purchased in a variety of lengths so they can be personalised to any square or rectangle to fit each project. To create your frame, simply slot the bars together at each corner. Where you place your drawing pins/thumb tacks is a matter of choice – on the front, side or back. I find that securing them on the back leads to fewer thread tangles, but everyone works slightly differently. (See page 21 for advice on framing up.)

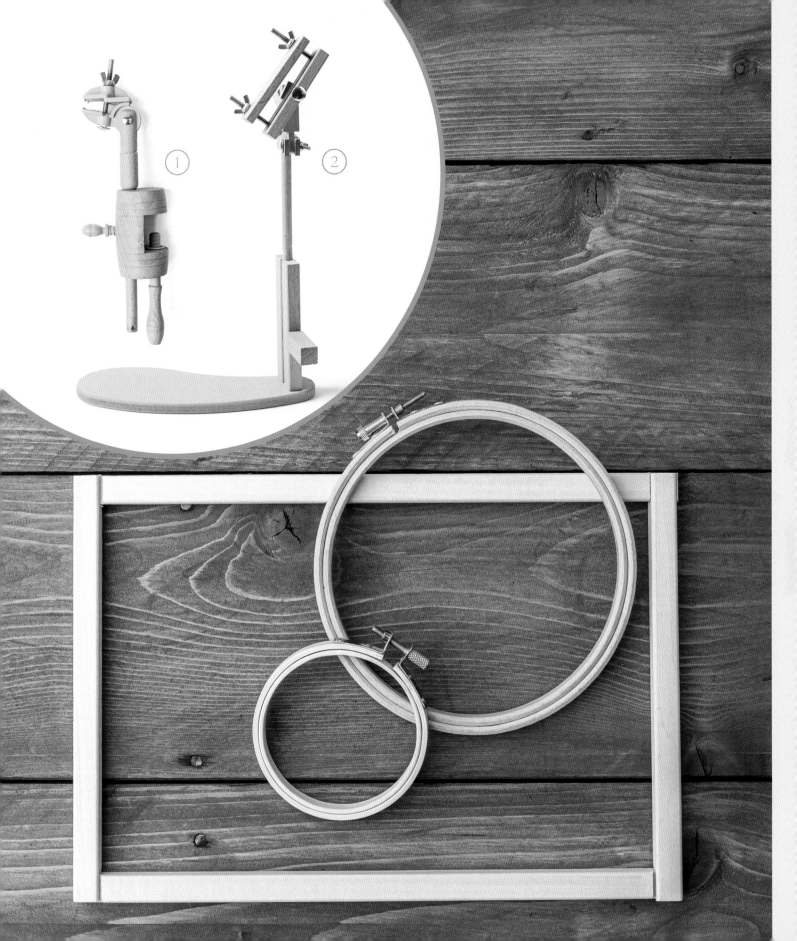

transferring the design

There are several different ways to transfer your design onto the fabric, and the method you choose will depend on many things such as the colour of your fabric and the time it will take you to complete your embroidery. I personally prefer to trace the design straight onto the fabric using an ordinary HB pencil.

PRICK AND POUNCE

This is a traditional method of transferring your design. Small holes are made in thick tracing paper along the design lines using a needle or a pricker. The paper is then laid on the fabric and a fine powder called pounce is rubbed over the image. The powder will fall through the holes onto the fabric leaving a trace of the design which can then be outlined in paint or pen by joining the dots.

TRANSFER PAPER

Transfer paper is very similar to carbon paper and comes in many different colours so can be useful for coloured fabrics. The transfer paper is placed between the design and the fabric, then the design is drawn over with a sharp pencil leaving a print on the fabric.

IRON-ON TRANSFER PENS AND PENCILS

Transfer pens can be useful for manmade fabrics such as polycotton, although marks can be permanent so the design will need to be covered by embroidery. The design is drawn over in reverse using the transfer pen and then placed, pen-side down, on the fabric and ironed. The image will transfer onto the fabric.

LIGHTBOX OR WINDOW

This is probably the easiest and quickest method of transferring your design and works best with thin, light fabric. I use a lightpad, which gives an even, bright light, but a sunny window will work very well too. Place your fabric over your design and place your frame over the top to check the image is in the correct position. Once it is positioned correctly you may wish to tape it in place to stop the fabric slipping. Simply trace over the design using an ordinary HB pencil or a fabric pen (see below).

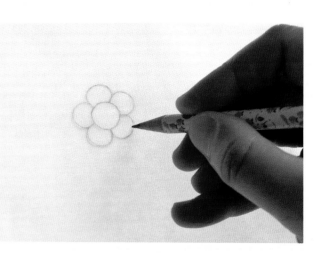

framing up

A bar frame

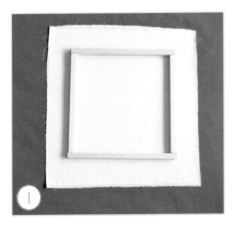 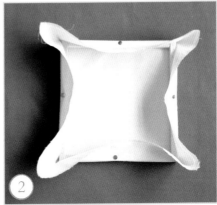 

STEP 1: Transfer your design (see opposite), then lay your fabric face down with the backing fabric on top. Centre your frame onto the backing fabric ensuring that there are a couple of inches (about 5cm) overlapping on all sides.

STEP 2: Pull the fabric reasonably tight over the frame and secure with one central drawing pin/thumb tack on each side. Turn your frame over to check that your design is central and straight.

STEP 3: Add more drawing pins/thumb tacks evenly along each side, pulling your fabric tight as you go. Check that your design remains central and does not become distorted – re-adjust the pins/tacks if necessary (you may need a screwdriver or blunt knife to remove them). Once you are happy that your fabric is drum-tight and correctly placed you may wish to trim some of the excess fabric from the back, as it can be quite easy to catch it accidentally when sewing.

A hoop

Loosen the screw on the outer hoop so that it will fit loosely over the inner. Lay your backing and main fabric over the inner hoop and press the outer hoop down over the top securing the fabric tightly between the two. Tighten the screw to keep the tension. You can hold your fabric over the steam from a kettle until just damp and allow it to dry to tighten your work further. You may wish to cover your work with a shower cap when you are not working on it to keep it clean and dust-free.

stretching and mounting

If you want to display your embroidery in a frame it will need to be removed from the hoop or bar frame and mounted. You can take it to a reputable framer who will be able to do this for you, but this can prove expensive, so you may want to do it yourself. Given the time it has taken you to create your embroidery it is important not to do anything at this stage that could ruin your work. Stay away from glue where possible, as this can stain your fabric and degrade over time, and try to use good-quality, acid-free mounting board or foam board. I have seen several different techniques for mounting embroidery, but this is the method that works for me.

You will need

Acid-free mounting board or foam board: the stronger the better
Extra-strong cotton thread
Strong pins
A needle, curved if possible, but a normal needle can be used
Calico or cotton fabric to cover the board if it is not the correct colour
A cutting board, metal ruler and sharp craft knife to cut the board to size

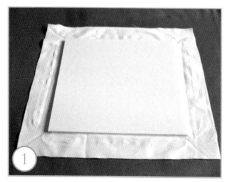

STEP 1: Work out what size you want your board, remembering that the frame will cover some of the area around the embroidery. I have used a piece of foam board that is approximately the same size as the bar frame the embroidery was worked on. If you are using mounting board, you may want to cut two pieces and stick them together – this not only strengthens the work and stops it bowing but also makes it easier to slip the pins into the side. You may want to cover your board with calico or cotton if the colour is likely to show through your fabric background. Lay your embroidery face down with the board centred on the reverse.

STEP 2: Fold each edge of the fabric over the board and secure with a central pin slid into the side. Once all four sides have been secured you can turn over your embroidery to check it is still central and straight, and adjust as necessary. When sliding the pins in, it can be tricky not to get the wrong angle and have the pin sticking out of the back or front; if this happens, correct it immediately as otherwise it could leave marks.

STEP 3: Add pins along all four sides, pulling the embroidery tight as you go. Keep checking that your work is still centred and straight with no puckering. I add even amounts of spaced-out pins on each side before filling in the gaps with more. If you find that there are places that are puckering, re-adjust and add more pins in the area to pull out the wrinkles.

STEP 4: To keep your corners neat so there is no stray fabric showing at the front, fold each corner rather like a bed sheet. Take the corner of the fabric and lay it across the back pointing to the centre of the board then fold each side of the fabric over, as shown in the photo.

STEP 5: Pin down your folded corners – this will allow you to have your hands free so that you can add a few stitches to pull the fabric together and hold it in position. Don't worry, this doesn't have to be pretty, as long as it holds your work.

STEP 6: Leaving the cotton on the reel, thread your needle. Start sewing long stitches across your work, rather like loosely lacing a corset; pass your needle through the fabric at each end, pulling the cotton through further. I can't use the same piece of thread all the way down as I get in a bit of a muddle, so when you have been back and forth a manageable amount of times, secure your thread. Then, go back and cut the thread from the reel leaving a decent amount to rethread your needle with back at the beginning. Pull your stitches tight, working from the bottom up to where your needle is, then secure the thread with a few stitches.

STEP 7: Once you have laced the embroidery all the way down you can remove the pins on those sides. Check the embroidery is smooth with no puckering – if there is a small wrinkle you can add some more stitches on the reverse to try to tighten the area.

STEP 8: Repeat steps six and seven, lacing the embroidery at right angles to your first set of stitches. Once all four sides have been laced, remove the remaining pins and check your embroidery is tight.

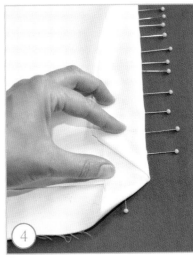

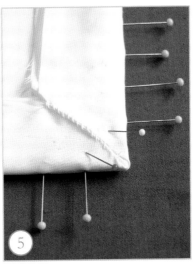

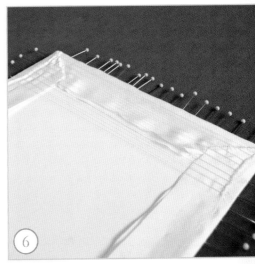

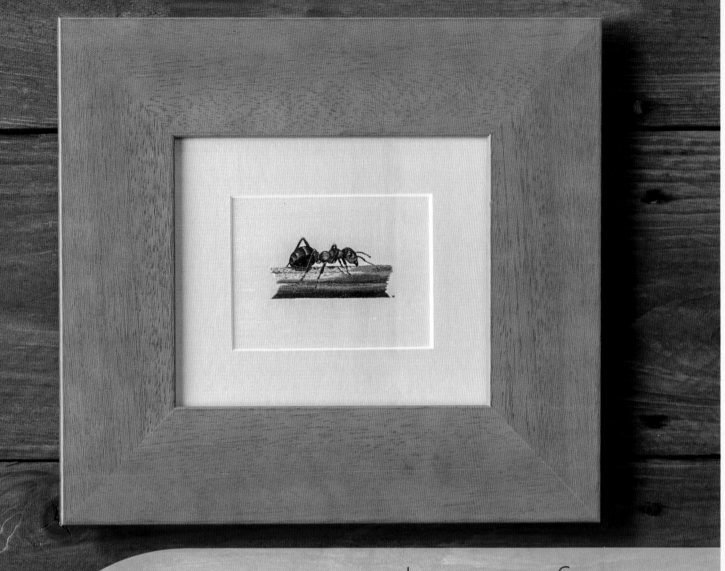

presentation of your embroidery

There are endless ways in which you can display your finished embroidery. If I have spent six months stitching a detailed piece of silk artwork I will usually have it professionally framed with non-reflective glass, with the intention of it being passed down through the generations. However, embroidery was traditionally used to decorate clothing and home furnishings, so why not think of different ways to finish your work and show it off to the world? A few different ideas are shown above and opposite to inspire you.

inspiration

Inspiration for your work can be taken from many different sources.
Looking at other people's embroidery on social media can be wonderful,
but needlepainting is an individual art and you should strive to find your
own style that reflects your interests and opinions.

Working from a photograph

I have always tried to work from my own photographs. This avoids any copyright issues and gives me a complete sense of ownership from start to finish. Working from a photograph has many benefits: the light stays the same, you can focus on small details as you sew and, probably most importantly, your subject stays completely still.

We are lucky to live in a time where access to a camera is easier than ever. Most of us have mobile/cell phones with a camera of some sort and this can come in handy as you never know when inspiration may hit. I can go out on a long walk with my expensive DSLR camera with the intention of taking beautiful reference photos and find nothing, but on the short walk to school with my daughter I have spotted snakes, beetles, slow worms and even a kingfisher! My mobile/cell phone may not be able to take as detailed a photograph but at least it is a reference.

Your photographs do not need to be award-winning pieces of art. If you choose to stitch insects it can be incredibly difficult to get a good picture as insects are very rarely still; just as you have lined up your shot they fly away. Just try taking a photograph of a bee and you will understand why they are referred to as busy. But what photographs can do is give us that basic inspiration to work from, and not everything in the photograph needs to go into your design – you can pick aspects from different pictures and work them together.

Sometimes your photograph will not be detailed enough, or an area of interest will not be visible. This is where I find other sources of information can be helpful. There are wonderful reference books available with detailed drawings or photographs of the plants or creatures you are interested in – even a quick internet search can bring up valuable information. However, it should always be remembered that these sources are someone else's hard work – use them as tools to aid your design, not as a source to be copied for commercial purposes.

Nature is an endless source of inspiration but it is important to remember that when taking photographs you should cause no damage, creatures should not be hurt in any way and flowers, unless you are sure of their conservation status, should not be picked. Do no harm.

Choosing your design

I used to think that if I could draw a subject then it followed that I could stitch it, but this unfortunately has not always proved to be true. Some aspects of a design may just be too detailed to translate into thread at the scale you want to work at (see the devil's-bit scabious, right, for example). That isn't to say that you must abandon the project, but certain details may need to be simplified.

Above: Devil's-bit scabious (*Succisa pratensis*).

Left: drawing of field bindweed (*Convolvulus arvensis*).

When you are looking through your photographs, try to imagine the stitches running through the image. Which way will they need to flow? Will the colours blend easily? Think of the light on the subject: where is the light source? If you can imagine yourself stitching it with confidence then it is a good sign that it will work.

You don't need to include every detail from your photograph; you may choose to merge several aspects of different images, taking an insect from one photograph and placing it on a flower from a different picture, for example. In the embroidery shown on page 132, I even stitched a spider on as an afterthought after a real one had dropped onto what I thought was a finished embroidery. If you are having trouble picturing the design in your head, you could trace the different aspects you like in each photograph and lay them over each other. Don't worry if you are not confident at drawing – I will sometimes trace the initial outline from my photograph and fill in the detail afterwards.

planning a design

Once you have your design and a basic template drawn you may feel a little bewildered as to where to start and how to tackle each detail. This is where a little pre-planning can give you the confidence to start stitching with a clear mind. You may find that as you become more experienced you don't always need to add these aids, but sometimes just going through them on paper can help to avoid mistakes later.

Stitch direction

The direction of your stitching is very important in needlepainting: it can add contour and veins to a leaf or a curve to a wasp's body. As there is no hard-and-fast rule about the direction you choose – I will often change my method from project to project – it is worth planning it out first.

Once you have created your template, think about the direction your stitching should take to create a three-dimensional effect; this will vary across different elements of your design. Add your stitch-direction lines to your template in a different colour – you can add as many as you like to help you with your embroidery. When I am transferring these lines onto the fabric I will often use a blue water-soluble embroidery pen, but a coloured pencil will also work as long as the marks will be completely covered by the finished embroidery.

If your design is of a leaf or a petal you may have an area in which some of the shape has turned over – this can create some confusion with your stitch-direction lines. To help understand the continuation of your lines it can help to sketch out the shape on paper, cut it out and draw the stitch lines on both sides. The area that is to be turned over can then be folded and the lines on the reverse will guide your design.

 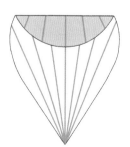

Shading guidelines

If you feel confident working straight from your coloured template or original photograph you may not need to add shading guidelines, but there are situations in which it can help to clarify a difficult shape. By adding lines to your design, in a different colour to your stitch direction, you can create a guide to the points at which the different colours will blend. Be careful that your template does not become too overcrowded with different guidelines as this can cause confusion and hinder rather than help your work. You should also be wary of becoming too regimented when stitching your shading rows, as this will create a hard line of colour: think of them as blending lines rather than points at which the colour must change.

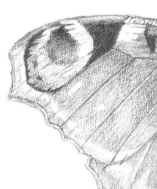

Ordering

Needlepainting should always be stitched 'back to front', so the details in the background are stitched before areas in the foreground. Sometimes this isn't always clear when sewing your design so it can be helpful to number your template with a stitching order. The petals of a flower are a useful example of this as some will sit behind others.

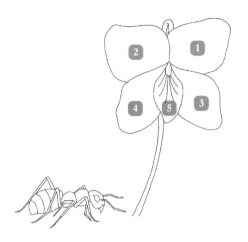

Colour guide

Once you have your design and template it can be very useful to create a colour guide. To put it simply, you colour your design in. If you originally worked from a photograph this can help to simplify the colours down and clarify them. I use everything from coloured pencils and acrylic paints to felt-tip pens to create a colour guide – it doesn't have to be a great work of art, as it is just for your own use. It can also help to create a tonal guide by photocopying your work in black and white, as this will help to clarify areas of light and shade without the confusion of colour.

Light direction

When you are planning your design it is important to work out where your light source is. In a photograph this may be obvious, but if you are designing a template from scratch you will need to imagine the position of the sun to highlight your design in a creative way. It is sometimes useful to draw the light source onto a template then follow the direction down and imagine where it will hit your subject. The hoverfly and ox-eye daisy (see right) is an interesting example, as each petal will have areas in both sunlight and shade and the hoverfly's body will create extra shade on the lower petals. Picturing your light source before you create your shading guide will give you a greater understanding of your work when you start sewing.

Choosing your threads

Matching threads to your design can be tricky. If you already have a large stash of threads it can be very enjoyable going through them matching each colour to your project, but if you are just starting out I would recommend seeing if your preferred thread brand sells a shade card. Buying thread from an image on the internet is not the same as seeing it in front of you.

Most companies will group their colours into families and it is worth looking at the whole family before deciding on the correct colours for your project; the shades within that family will naturally follow on from each other so you know they will blend smoothly.

Try to match your threads in natural daylight as artificial light can change the appearance of the colour. Silk floss can sometimes appear darker when viewed without the direct light source of your magnifying lamp, and colours that seemed bright and vibrant when you were stitching will appear rather dark when the lamp is taken away. It is worth making use of the lightest and darkest shades within each colour group for a harmonious contrast.

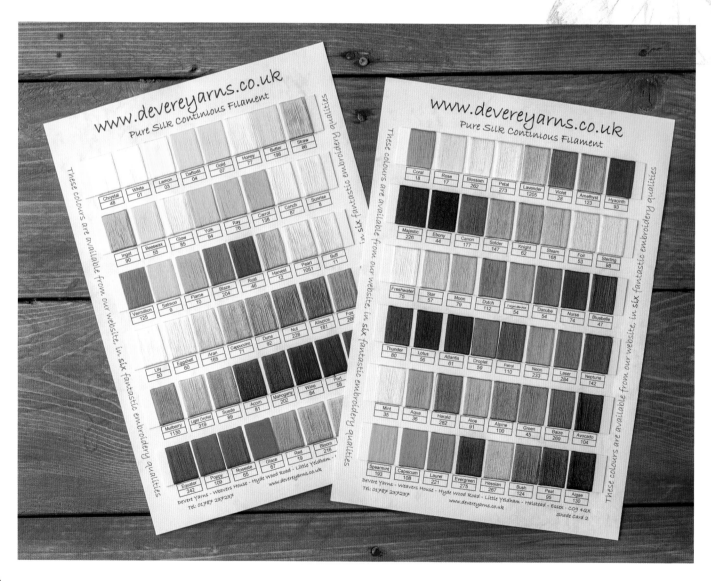

needlepainting

Needlepainting, or silk shading, is a very free style of embroidery. There are no set rules and it is this sense of improvization that can result in some of the most vibrant and stunning embroideries.

Although needlepainting can be a very individual skill, a basic knowledge of some of the main stitches is a useful tool. I would encourage anyone just starting out to practise basic techniques and shapes first before going on to create their own style and way of stitching. There are many useful books and videos out there that can help you on your journey; in my experience, most of these guides vary slightly according to the author's preferred style, but the ideas are generally the same across them all.

Over the following pages I will show you the basic methods I use to create my work, however, it is worth saying again that once you have learnt these basic techniques you should not be afraid to then adapt them all! I like to work with very small stitching while others prefer to use long threads; I won't always work in rows of shade, I will work up and down the shape or fill small areas dotted around the image instead of working in one place. I have used silk floss in these guides as it is my preferred thread, however you may

choose to use cotton. It really is up to you: just take your time and have fun with it.

The main technique used in silk shading is long-and-short stitch (see pages 32–35). This is such a versatile way of sewing, allowing you to create flow and movement while blending colours to give your work a sense of depth. It generally has a very flat appearance, so the addition of alternative stitches can add variety and texture to your work. Different stitches need to be used sparingly to ensure that they enhance the thread painting and don't detract from it. Adding French knots to the centre of a flower or lazy-daisy stitches to create the feathery leaves of cow parsley can add interest and make your work stand out. There are many books out there that can guide you through the dizzying multitude of stitches available, but the following pages cover some basic techniques that will help you if you want to try the projects in this book.

Basic long-and-short stitch

A great place to start your long-and-short stitch journey is tapestry shading, where the stitches will always travel in a vertical direction. This will get you used to laying stitches directly next to each other and continuing colours to create a smooth appearance. This is a very basic shape with lines to indicate roughly the length of your stitching and the points where the colours will change. I have used contrasting colours to clearly show the different layers of stitching. The size of the template I have given, right, is approximately 3 x 2cm (1¼ x ¾in).

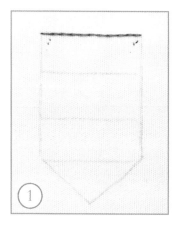

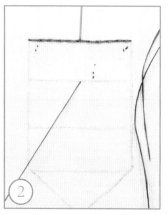

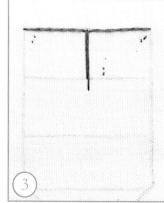

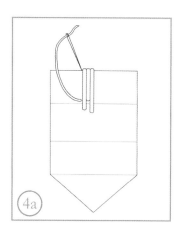

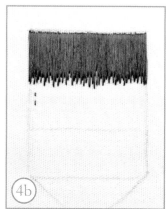

STEP 1: To create a crisp edge to your shape it is best to start by sewing a line of split stitch (see page 37) along the top edge using a matching colour. Start with a waste knot (see page 37) and two stitches in an area that will be covered by embroidery. In this shape the sides will not need to be outlined as your stitches will lie vertically down and not have to tuck over an edge. Finish with two stitches in an area to be covered by embroidery (see page 37).

STEP 2: Using a new thread, start in the centre of your first row of stitching and bring your needle up through the fabric at the point of the first shading line, this does not necessarily need to be exactly on the line, as all your stitches will vary in length. Take your needle back down through the fabric just over the top of the line of split stitch – this should be directly above the point at which your needle came up. This stitch should be as vertical as possible, lying 90 degrees to your line of split stitch, as it will guide the angle of the rest of the stitches in this row.

STEP 3: Bring your needle back up through the fabric directly next to your first stitch but at either a higher or lower point. As before, take your needle back down through the fabric just over the line of split stitch. You should not be able to see the fabric between your stitches. If you can, it would be best to either pull the thread out and re-sew it, or add a stitch in between, but be careful to make sure it is a different length to the two threads either side.

STEP 4: Continue sewing stitches of varying lengths along the row to the end then return to the centre and work to the opposite side. Ensure that there are no stitches laying next to each other that are the same length, and check for any gaps where fabric can be seen.

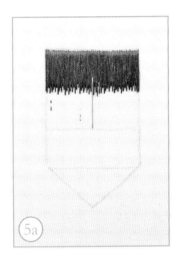
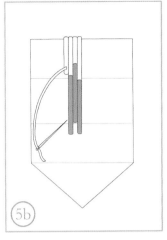
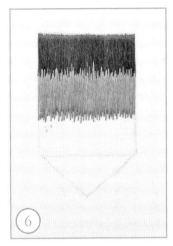
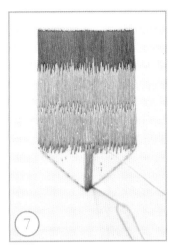

STEP 5: Your second row of shading will again start in the centre, but this time your needle will come up through the stitch in the previous row, splitting the thread. It will then be taken down through the fabric around the point of the second shading line. While the first row of stitches all varied in length, the second row will all be a similar length to each other, as their end point will be determined by the stitch in the previous row. Splitting the stitches in the previous row helps to anchor the thread.

STEP 6: As with your first row of shading, continue your stitches to one edge then return to the centre and work the other way. All your stitches will be a similar length but will vary in their placement according to the stitching in the first row.

STEP 7: Repeat steps 5 and 6 to complete the row containing the third thread colour. Before sewing the fourth and final row you will need to split stitch the pointed bottom line. Your final row of stitching will be similar to your first – the starting point of each stitch will vary according to the previous row but the thread will be taken down through the fabric as close to the line of split stitch as possible.

STEP 8: Once your stitching is complete you may have small holes where the needle has split the previous stitch. To help close these holes, run your needle over your work as if combing the thread – this will also help to blend the floss and give your embroidery a smoother appearance.

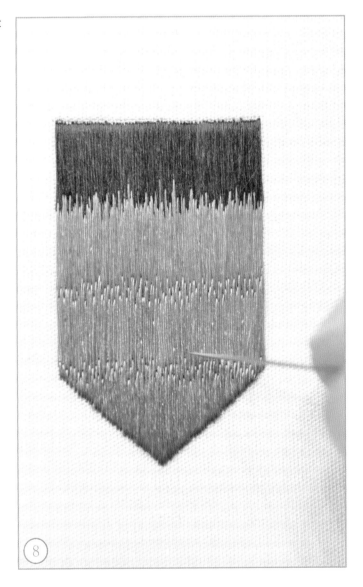

Directional long-and-short stitch

The wonderful thing about needlepainting is the lifelike effect that can be created with the freedom to follow the shape and flow of a subject. Stitches will increase and decrease as necessary and the colours will gently blend into each other to create subtle shading. A perfect practice example of this stitch variation is a petal. If you look closely, a petal has faint veins that taper to a point as the colour often blends from one shade to another.

I have used a basic petal shape and added stitch-direction lines in blue with shading guidelines in red. Use any colour thread you like, but try to find three shades that will blend into each other and not create too much of a contrast. The size of the template I have given is 3 x 2cm (1¼ x ¾in).

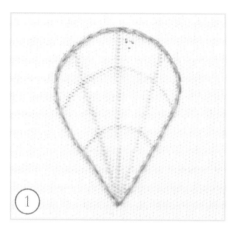

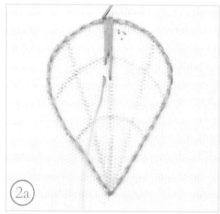

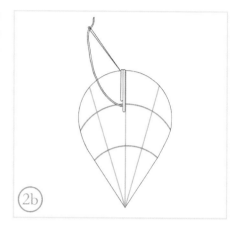

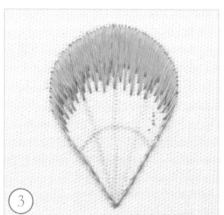

STEP 1: Starting with one of the shades in your project (I have used my darkest pink but you may choose to use a different shade), split stitch the outline of the shape all the way around (see page 37). Use a waste knot (see page 37) to start and finish your thread in an area that will be covered by the embroidery stitches.

STEP 2: As with basic long-and-short stitch, you will start in the centre of your shape. Bring your needle up through the fabric around the first shading line then take it back down just over the top of the split-stitch outline. As I want the colours to blend smoothly I have used stitches of greatly varying lengths. The first few stitches have been placed alongside each other, but you will need to start gradually changing the angle of your sewing. This can be achieved by bringing the needle up through the fabric directly below the point at which your previous stitch began and then taking it back down over your split stitch alongside the thread at the top. This will very subtly change the direction of your stitching.

STEP 3: Continue stitching along the top row, gradually changing the direction of your stitching every now and then to make sure that you are meeting your direction line. Not every stitch will need to be angled; the more you practise, the more you will get a feel for the change of direction that is needed for each shape.

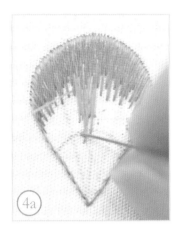  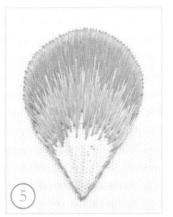 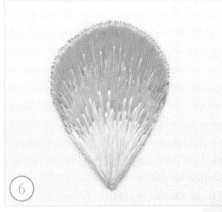

STEP 4: Your second row of stitching will follow a similar pattern but, as with basic long-and-short stitch, you will be bringing your needle up through the previous thread, splitting it. To change the angle of your stitching you can either take your needle down directly below the thread in the previous row or you can tuck it slightly behind the stitch next to it using your needle to temporarily push it to one side. As you change the angle you will find that the number of stitches decreases, and you will not need to split every single stitch in the previous row.

STEP 5: The length of your stitches in this row will all be roughly the same but the point at which you bring your needle up can vary. If you feel that the colours are not smoothly blending, bring your needle up further into the previous row from time to time, creating a stitch that reaches further up into the previous shade.

STEP 6: The final row of shading culminates in a point, however, if all your stitches end at that point it will become overcrowded and bulky. Use the same method of decreasing stitches as the previous rows, with just a few evenly spaced threads on each side reaching down to the point. Your stitches at the side will need to cover your outline so you may like to work a couple of threads that start on the outside of the shape but end just inside.

Parking your needles

Sometimes when you are needlepainting you will be changing threads frequently as you blend different colours in a small area. Tying off your thread and starting a new one each time you change colour can be time-consuming and a waste of floss so, if you feel confident, it can help to have several needles threaded up and ready to go at the same time. Keeping threads ready to go in an area away from your embroidery is sometimes called 'parking your needle'. Some people prefer to have their thread at the back of their work with the needle reaching round and parked at the front but I like to have all my floss in view so I don't get it tangled. Try different ways and see which works best for you.

If you have finished a small area of colour but you still have plenty of thread and you know you will be returning to it very shortly, bring your needle to the front in the area in which it will next be needed. With the floss pulled completely through and out of the way of your work, find an area to leave your needle at the edge of the fabric so as not to leave any visible holes when the work is mounted and framed. When the thread is needed again, pick up your needle and take it through to the back, ready to start stitching again.

Parking needles can leave you in a tangle if you are trying it for the first time, but once you have discovered your favourite method and needle positioning, it can really help to save time and floss.

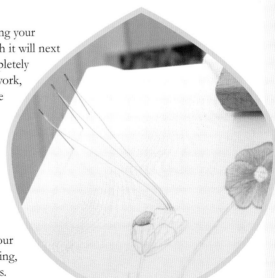

additional stitches

Threading your needle

Using silk floss or one strand of cotton thread requires you to use a relatively small needle, however, small needles have small eyes and threading them can be tricky. There are various techniques for threading a needle and everyone has their own preference. The method I like to use takes a little practice, but once you have mastered it threading your needle takes no time at all.

Firstly, make sure that the end of your thread has been snipped straight across with sharp embroidery scissors – any straggly, fluffy bits will make it impossible to thread. Pinch the thread between your thumb and forefinger so that it is nearly hidden. Hold the eye of the needle over the end of the thread and gradually slide it down between your fingers while at the same time rolling your fingers upwards, exposing more of the floss.

Quick knot

I use a very quick and simple technique to tie my knots; they don't have to be pretty as they will eventually be snipped off.

STEP 1: Pinch your thread between your thumb and forefinger with the thread pointing upwards. Wrap the thread around your finger once, bringing it back to the upward position (you will now have two parts of the thread between your thumb and forefinger).

STEP 2: Slide your finger down your thumb, rolling the two pieces of thread together and off.

STEP 3: Bring in your second finger and slide the tangled thread down so it clumps in a knot at the bottom.

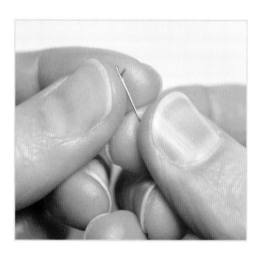

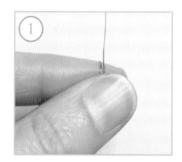

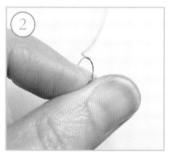

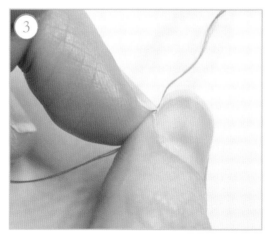

Waste knot

This is one of the most useful techniques I have learned; this simple technique will leave your work smooth and knot-free.

STEP 1: After tying a knot in your floss, find an area next to where you will begin stitching but make sure it is a place that will eventually be covered in embroidery. Take your needle down through the fabric leaving the knot on the top.

STEP 2: Bring your needle up through the fabric near to your starting point, sew two tiny stitches, then bring your needle up at the point at which you will start sewing.

STEP 3: Start sewing and, when the thread is secure, go back and snip off the knot.

Finishing your thread

Finishing the thread after sewing is done in a very similar way to creating a waste knot (above). Sew two tiny stitches near to your finishing point in an area that will eventually be covered in embroidery, bring your thread through to the front and simply snip it off.

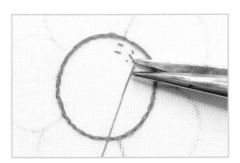

Split stitch

Split stitch is quite possibly my favourite sewing technique. I use it in nearly all my work and find it the most versatile stitch for needlepainting. It can be used to create a crisp outline that can then be stitched over with satin or long-and-short stitch, giving it a defined, slightly raised edge. Or it can be used in single lines for a variety of designs, for stalks or insect limbs and antennae or even as a filler stitch for larger areas such as the spathe of the lords-and-ladies plant on page 56.

STEP 1: Start your thread with a waste knot, then bring your needle up from underneath the fabric at your starting point. Take your needle back down according to the size of stitch you want.

STEP 2: Bring your needle up through the middle of the first stitch, splitting the thread in two.

STEP 3: Take the needle back down alongside to create your next stitch, which should be a similar size to your first. Continue in the same way, bringing your needle up through the previous stitch as you work along the line.

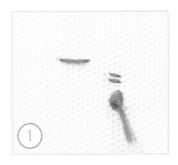

Satin stitch

Satin stitch can be used to fill small areas where it may be difficult to use long-and-short stitch. I will quite often use it if there is a small area of a leaf or petal that has turned over to show the underside – the satin stitch can be angled to follow the same stitch direction set out in your long-and-short stitch and continue to add to the impression of veins and flow.

It can be tricky at first to keep all stitches laying directly next to each other without allowing the fabric to show through. Try to keep your tension the same throughout the shape as this will help to make sure that some threads don't appear bulky and loose while others are so tight they can distort the fabric.

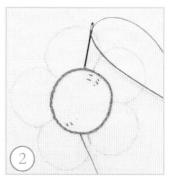
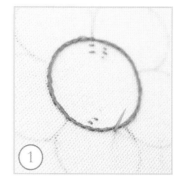
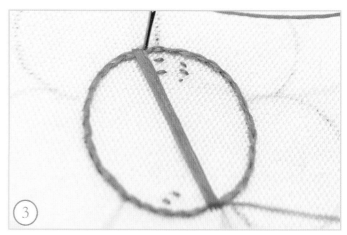

STEP 1: Split stitch around the shape in the same colour you are going to use to fill it (see page 37); this will help to give a nice crisp edge to your satin stitch. Bring your needle up outside the split-stitch outline in a central position.

STEP 2: Take your needle back down over the split stitch outline directly opposite the point at which you brought your needle up. Make sure that your needle rests above the split stitch and doesn't pull the outline thread out of shape.

STEP 3: Repeat steps 1 and 2, bringing your needle up and taking it down as close to the first stitch as possible. This stitch and all subsequent stitches should lie at the same angle and directly next to the previous one. If your stitch is not at the correct angle or you can see fabric between the stitches it may be best to re-stitch it or add a stitch in any gaps. Work your way across, filling in one side of the shape, then return to the centre and fill in the other side.

The completed area of satin stitch should have a smooth, glossy appearance.

French knots

French knots can add a great texture to your work – they can appear very structured and tactile when clustered together. I have used French knots to create textured effects like moss and the centres of flowers (see page 64).

If you are using cotton thread, the size of your knot will depend on how many strands of floss you have in your needle, however, silk can be a little trickier. I have found that silk floss can be so fine that the knot is too small and gets pulled back through the fabric, but that isn't to say it is impossible. If you take it slowly and don't pull your thread too hard it can be done. I will usually wind my thread around the needle more than once to make a slightly larger knot.

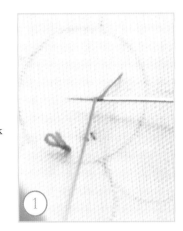

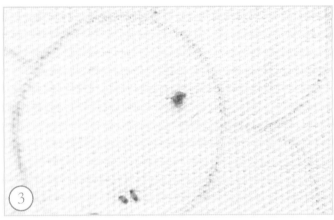

STEP 1: Bring your thread fully through to the front of the fabric and wind it around your needle. In this photograph I have wound the floss around the needle once to demonstrate how small the knot will be with silk.

STEP 2: Pull your thread tight and take your needle back down into the fabric very closely to the point at which it came up. Do not put it in the same hole or your knot will just pull straight through the fabric.

STEP 3: Pull the thread through while controlling it on top – don't let go of the floss on top until you are sure it won't tangle.

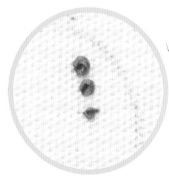

When I want larger knots using silk floss I will wind the thread around the needle two or three times. In this photograph you can see the difference in size between one, two and three turns around the needle.

When French knots are tightly packed together they can create a wonderful texture, perfect for flowers such as daisies where the centre is full of tiny florets.

Seed stitch

Seed stitch can be used to fill areas and create the appearance of texture; you can also vary the shade of thread and density of stitching. I often find it useful to fill the centre of flowers with seed stitch, as it gives the suggestion of pollen and anthers.

STEP 1: Bring your thread to the front of the fabric and take it back down a short distance away, creating a small stitch. Repeat these small stitches at varying angles to each other.

STEP 2: Fill the area with small stitches, making sure they are all at different angles to each other. You can change the spacing between the stitches to give a denser appearance.

Lazy-daisy stitch

Also known as daisy stitch, lazy daisy is very useful for fine feathered plants when a mass of tiny petals is too intricate for long-and-short or satin stitch. It has a very delicate appearance and can also be used as tiny wings on insects that are far too small to show any detail (see page 56).

STEP 1: Bring your thread fully through to the front of the fabric then take your needle back down as close to that point as possible. Do not pull your thread all the way back through.

STEP 2: Without pulling your thread all the way through, bring your needle back up through the fabric according to the size you would like your stitch to be. Catch the loop of floss that has been left on top with your needle and then pull your thread through. This will tighten your floss, leaving a small loop on top of the fabric.

STEP 3: Take your needle back down through the fabric on the other side of the thread, creating a small stitch that will hold your loop in place.

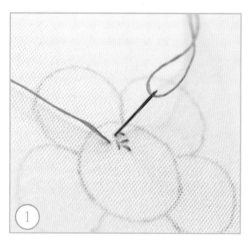

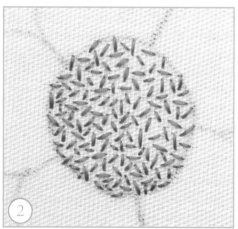

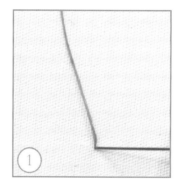

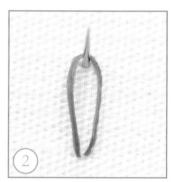

small stitched elements

Sewing small shaped elements can help you hone your skills,
so here are a few examples to get you started.

Ladybird shell

A ladybird shell, also called an elytra, provides a perfect opportunity to practise stitch direction and shine; the direction lines are slightly rounded and do not all meet at the top. This template shows stitch direction lines in blue and a rough guide to the layers of shading in red. I decided to use orange threads/floss, but use any colour you want. Make sure your three shades blend smoothly so the colour change is not too jarring. The actual size of the template is 2 x 1cm (¾ x ½in).

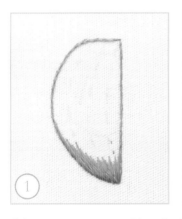
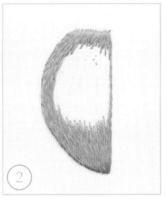
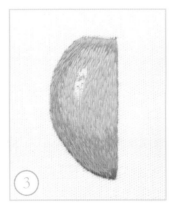
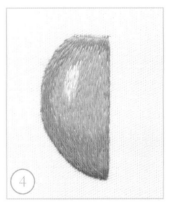

STEP 1: Outline the shell in split stitch using one of your chosen shades (I used the darkest). Starting from the bottom, I find it helpful to split stitch up the shading guidelines first, as this will give a better idea of how the stitches will need to increase. Some of your first stitches can meet at the same place in the bottom point, but not all, or it will become too crowded. As your stitches reach out towards the left of the shell they will no longer be stretching all the way back to your starting point, but will instead gradually work their way up the side.

STEP 2: Your second shade will continue up the side of the shell and start coming down from the top. Try to cover your split-stitch outline with this shade, changing the direction of your stitches as you work

back in towards the top. If you have used a darker shade to outline the shape it doesn't matter too much if this shows a little, as it can add depth.

STEP 3: Fill the remaining area, apart from the highlight, with your lightest shade. I have left the darker outline showing on the straight edge as it helps add definition.

STEP 4: Fill the remaining section with white and try to stretch some stitches further into your lightest shade so that it blends in rather than being a defined line. Remember to run the point of your needle over your stitching to close any holes.

Berry

Berries are my favourite shape to sew. Apart from the fact that autumn is my favourite season, I love the light and dark, the heavy shading in the area furthest from the sun and then the dash of white that just gives it the 'ta-da!' moment and brings it to life.

Berries come in all shapes, sizes and colours so I have chosen a simple ball shape, rather like a hawthorn berry. I have experimented with different stitch directions in the past to find the best shading method and I have found that working in a sort of beachball pattern creates the best effect, with stitches fanning out from a central point such as the stalk or the tip of the berry. I have added stitch-direction lines in blue and shading guidelines in red. The actual size of the template is 1.5 x 1.5cm (⅝ x ⅝ in).

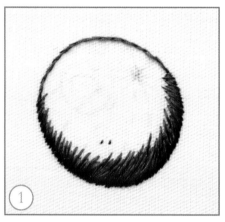
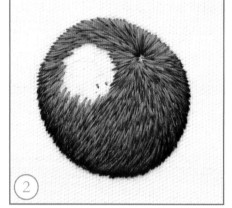
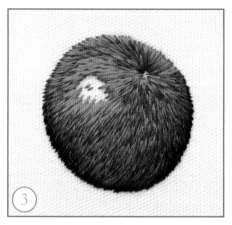

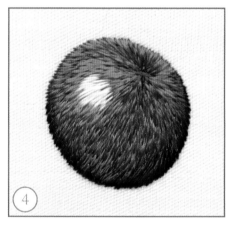

STEP 1: Starting with your darkest shade, split stitch the outline of the berry. Working on the central stitch-direction line first (the one that is straight), start working long-and-short stitch around the edge of your berry in the darkest shaded area. You will find that the angle of your stitching becomes more extreme as you work your way around. You will need to keep your stitches small at either end of this shaded area and work more than one row in the centre. Be careful about the placement of your stitches outside the shape as a stitch in the wrong place can start to change the shape of your berry. If you feel a stitch is in the wrong place it may be best to take it out and re-stitch.

STEP 2: Continue your stitching in your next shade and carry on working around the berry. Where your stitches meet at the tip, you will need to leave a small area free of thread. Don't finish all your floss at this central point or it will become too crowded.

STEP 3: Carry on shading in your lightest colour, leaving only a small area to add the shine. Some stitches will extend into the highlight to make sure that the colours blend and the change of shade is not too dramatic.

STEP 4: Fill the remaining area in white to create the point at which the light is directly shining on the berry. Using a dark brown floss, add four stitches crossing over each other at the tip of the berry – this will cover the area not filled with stitching and create the point where the flower originally was before the berry developed.

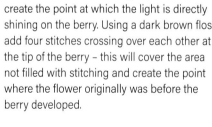

Leaf

Leaves can vary greatly in shape, colour and texture, and how you choose to stitch them can change from project to project. Light direction will play an important part in your shading; both sides of the leaf may follow the same shading pattern or be opposite, or the shading may change halfway down. Creating a shading guide using coloured pencils before you start can be a great help.

I have used a basic leaf template and kept the light source coming from above so the shading will work from dark to light on one side and light to dark on the other. I have drawn the vein lines in black and the stitch direction lines, which follow the veins, in blue. The actual size of the template is 3 x 2.5cm (1¼ x 1in).

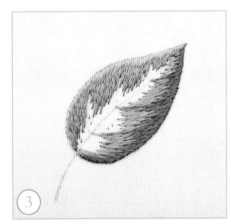

STEP 1: Outline the edge of the first side of the leaf in split stitch using the appropriate green. Start your first row of long-and-short stitch using your stitch-direction and vein lines. I find it helpful to work down the vein lines in the darkest green to create the impression of indentation and to help guide the stitches. I like to use small stitches, so I have worked more than one row of dark green, especially around the veins. You may choose to use longer stitches so may only need one row. The angle of your stitches will need to change subtly at the top and bottom of the leaf.

STEP 2: The opposite side of the leaf will start with light green, as I have placed the light source directly above. Split stitch the outline in your lightest shade of green then work long-and-short stitch as before. As the veins will still be the darkest part of the leaf, I have worked the stitching down further in between each vein.

STEP 3: The middle rows of stitching on both sides will be medium green. Continue your shading following the patterns set out previously, trying to keep the veins as the darkest areas.

STEP 4: Fill the remaining areas on both sides: use your lightest green on the bottom half and darkest green on the top. For the stalk and central vein I have used medium green; I have stitched two rows of split stitch for the stalk to give it some thickness and continued one of the lines down the centre of the leaf. Some leaves may have darker or lighter veins.

the projects

The projects in this book aim to represent the main groups of pollinators: flies, beetles, moths, butterflies, bees (other than honeybees) and wasps. Each insect is presented alongside a plant that it is either attracted to and helps pollinate or that can be found in a similar habitat.

I have provided step-by-step photographs of the process I used to create each embroidery but don't feel that you must copy this to the stitch. You may like to focus on individual aspects of a project or try different embroidery styles and colours. If you are new to needlepainting, you may like to try a small area of a project before attempting a whole design. If you would prefer to use cotton instead of silk floss you may need to enlarge the template slightly due to the thickness of the thread.

For each project I have provided a descriptive name for each colour used and a reference to the specific thread and supplier in case you want to create the same effect.

I have also supplied a guide to stitch direction, shading and ordering for each project to help you if needed.

Needlepainting is a slow process but the results can be incredibly satisfying, so don't be put off if this is the first time you have tried it – with patience anything can be achieved.

Dog Rose and Greenbottle Fly

Rosa canina and *Lucilia caesar*

DOG ROSE

During spring these beautiful, delicate roses can be seen climbing and entwining themselves through sunny hedgerows and the margins of woodland. Ordinarily the dog rose can climb to about 5m (16½ft) in height, but it can scramble up trees far higher using its curved thorns to cling and support its growth. Flowers within the *Canina* family have five petals varying in colour from deep pink to near white and have a subtle, sweet scent.

The name 'dog rose' is thought to have come from the shape of the thorns, which are like dogs' teeth, but also from its classical use, as recorded by the Roman naturalist Pliny, for the treatment of a bite from a mad dog. Common names include wild rose, briar rose, dog berry and witches briar.

The flowers are an important nectar source for pollinating insects and the fruits provide food for birds in the autumn. The hips of the dog rose are also an excellent source of vitamin C for humans, having four times the amount of blackcurrants and twenty times that of orange juice. In the UK during the Second World War, people were encouraged to collect rosehips to make syrup when supplies of citrus fruit were cut off. The syrup can be used as a flavouring for ice cream and milk puddings or diluted as a drink. When making the syrup it is important to filter out the seeds as they are covered in little hairs which can be a dangerous internal irritant (in the past, children would often save the seeds to use as itching powder).

GREENBOTTLE FLY

The shock of green glistening in the sun can be like glimpsing a rare gem within your garden, although the greenbottle fly is often just seen as a pest that spreads disease. Perhaps it is time we look at these little treasures in a different light.

Measuring between 8 and 15mm (⅓ – ⅔in), the adult greenbottle fly is classed as a true fly with only one pair of wings, short antennae and large compound eyes. It will often visit flowers to feed on nectar and pollen and can play an important part in the pollination process. Some plants have even adapted to specifically attract this group of pollinators and developed a strong smell that imitates rotting flesh. While greenbottle flies are often attracted to strong, pungent smelling plants they will happily feed on the fruit and nectar from many flowers. They can be found in a variety of different habitats such as gardens and woodlands, where they can often be spotted sunning themselves in patches of dappled light and are important to the balance of a healthy ecosystem.

A member of the blowfly family, greenbottles lay their eggs on carrion and decomposing animal matter, and the larvae will go on to feed on the rotting flesh. The name blowfly comes from the old belief that they would somehow blow their eggs onto the rotting meat. While the presence of blowflies is a concern around livestock and needs to be addressed, their ability to help with the decomposition process means that if they were to disappear overnight, the world would soon pile up with a layer of rotting flesh. Forensic entomologists can even determine the time of death at a crime scene by studying the larval stage of blowfly development.

While the thought of the greenbottle larvae feeding on dead flesh may seem like something from a horror story, this process has been utilized in medicine for centuries and is even still used today. Greenbottle maggots bred in a sterile environment will be used on wounds where they will eat the dead tissue and leave the healthy; they will also kill bacteria and stimulate new growth. It is a process that human practice has never been able to achieve to the same effectiveness.

Threads used

I have used Pipers Silks floss silks for this project

FOR THE FLY

Dark green-blue – Pipers 'Tartan'
Medium green-blue – Pipers 'Green Blue'
Light green-blue – Pipers 'Pastel Green'
Light yellow-green – Pipers 'Moss'
White – Pipers 'White'
Black – Pipers 'Black'
Light grey – Pipers 'Light Grey'
Orange-brown – Pipers 'Henna'

FOR THE FLOWER

Dark pink – Pipers 'Cyclamen'
Medium pink – Pipers 'China Rose'
Light pink – Pipers 'Heather Pink'
Very pale pink – Pipers 'Pale Pink'
Dark yellow – Pipers 'King Cup'
Medium yellow – Pipers 'Light Gold'
Orange-brown – Pipers 'Henna'

FOR THE ROSEHIPS

Dark red – Pipers 'Mid Cardinal'
Medium red – Pipers 'Kenya Red'
Light red – Pipers 'Po Red'
Brown – Pipers 'Brown'
Very pale pink – Pipers 'Pale Pink'

FOR THE STEM AND LEAVES

Brown – Pipers 'Brown'
Dark green – Pipers 'Forest Green'
Medium green – Pipers 'Leaf'
Light green – Pipers 'Pale Leaf'

Template: page 136

Stitches used

Long-and-short stitch (page 32)
Split stitch (page 37)
Satin stitch (page 38)
Seed stitch (page 40)
French knots (page 39)

Shading guide

Stitch-direction guide

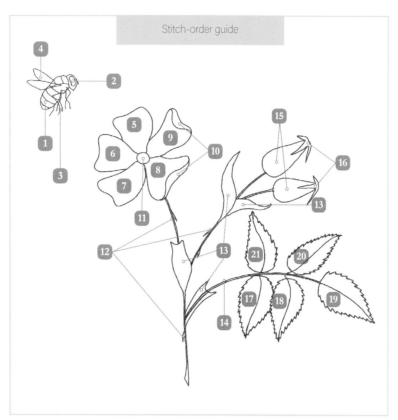

Stitch-order guide

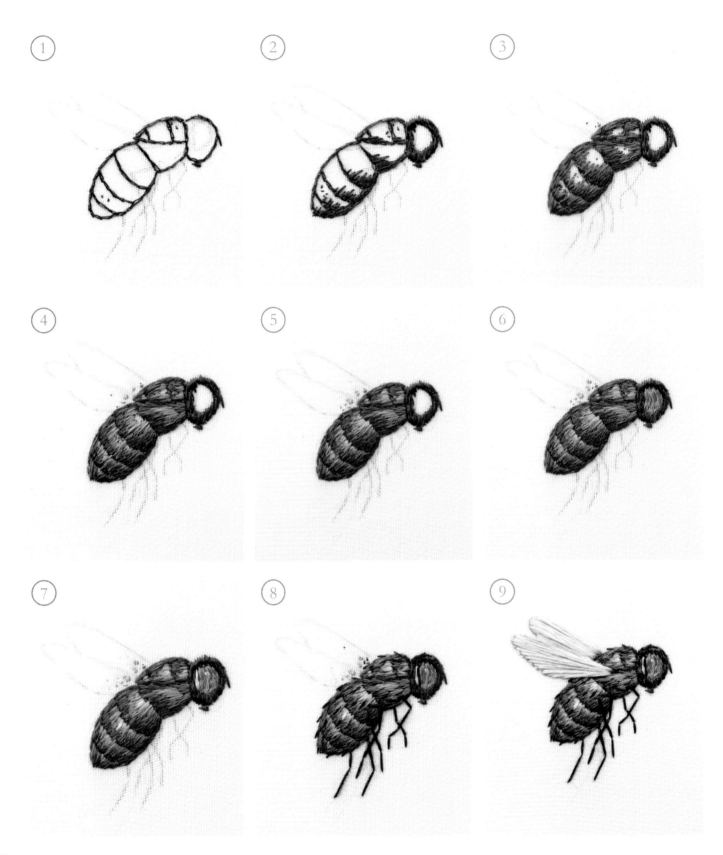

How to stitch

STEP 1: Outline the body and sections of the fly in split stitch using dark green-blue (Tartan). Add a small stitch for the mouth and antenna.

STEP 2: Using dark green-blue (Tartan), stitch around the eye in split stitch. Shade each section in long-and-short stitch as in the photograph, working up and down the body. The shading should be heavier on the lower side to reflect the direction of the light.

STEP 3: Using medium green-blue (Green Blue) continue the shading of each section.

STEP 4: Continue to shade with light green-blue (Pastel Green).

STEP 5: Fill the remaining body sections with light yellow-green (Moss).

STEP 6: Fill the eye with orange-brown (Henna). I have used curving lines of split stitch, but you may prefer to sew the area in satin stitch.

STEP 7: Using white (White), highlight around and in the eye. Add a stitch within each area of light yellow-green on the body to add a highlight.

STEP 8: Stitch the legs and hairs using black (Black). Try to think about the positioning of the legs, and therefore which threads should be in the background and which in the foreground. You can also add some black to areas around the eye to add definition.

STEP 9: Using light grey (Light Grey) sew long stitches for the wings. Start with the furthest wing, then sew the front wing. Not all stitches need to run the entire length of the wing as they will overlap to form the point. If all stitches ran the full length of the wing the threads would become too clustered at the point.

STEP 10: Starting with the first petal, outline the shape in split stitch using medium pink (China Rose). Then shade the area in long-and-short stitch, following the stitch direction lines, working from medium pink (China Rose) to light pink (Heather Pink) then very pale pink (Pale Pink).

STEP 11: Repeat step 10 with all the petals, using the order guide on page 49. Stitch the petal turn-overs in satin stitch using dark pink (Cyclamen).

STEP 12: Fill the centre of the rose with seed stitches (see page 40) in dark yellow (King Cup) and medium yellow (Light Gold). Extend long stitches in medium yellow of varying lengths along the petals and finish each stitch with a French knot (see page 39) in orange-brown (Henna).

STEP 13: Using brown (Brown), split stitch the stems and thorns. The thorns can be sewn using three to four simple stitches forming a triangle with one longer stitch pointing down. The lower stem should preferably be stitched after the joining leaf as it is in the foreground.

STEP 14: The smaller joining leaves are sewn in satin stitch (see page 38) using medium green (Leaf) and light green (Pale Leaf). A central vein can be added to the upper joining leaf in medium green.

STEP 15: Complete the lower stem using split stitch in brown (Brown). Using dark red (Mid Cardinal), outline the rosehips and start shading; the stitch direction lines can be added for guidance. Keep in mind the light direction – the heaviest shading will be at the bottom.

STEP 16: Add medium red (Kenya Red) as the next shade.

STEP 17: Light red (Po Red) fills most of the remaining space, followed by very pale pink (Pale Pink) to add the shine where the light source hits the berry directly.

STEP 18: Use long stitches of brown (Brown) in varying lengths to create a point on the withered sepals of the rosehips. The side sepals should be stitched first, followed by the central area.

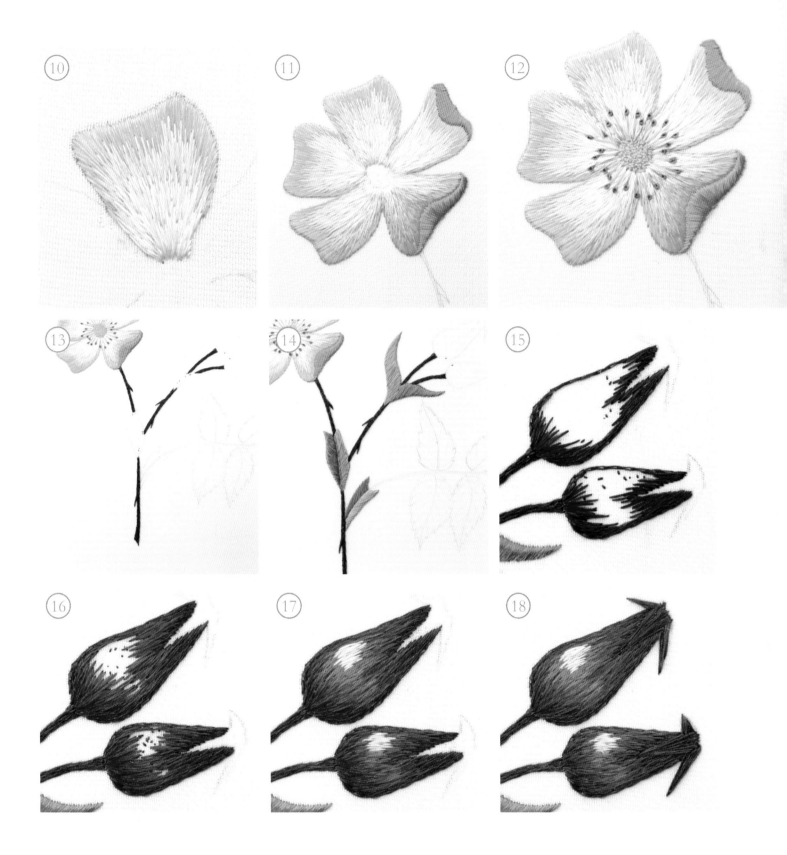

STEP 19: Outline the left-hand side of the first leaf in dark green (Forest Green) and, following the stitch guidelines, sew the outer edge in long-and-short stitch. The stitches can extend towards the centre to form the veins.

STEP 20: Sew the next row of shading in medium green (Leaf). Follow the veins on to the centre of the leaf.

STEP 21: Fill the remaining area of this side of the leaf with light green (Pale Leaf).

STEP 22: Repeat steps 19, 20 and 21 on the right-hand side of the leaf, but this time working from light to dark. If you have used the stitch-direction lines to form your veins, the light green stitches on the outer edge will this time need to extend towards the centre between the veins (see page 43).

STEP 23: Stitch all the remaining leaves using the same process and following the shading guide. A line of split stitch in light green (Pale Leaf) is added to each leaf to represent the central vein.

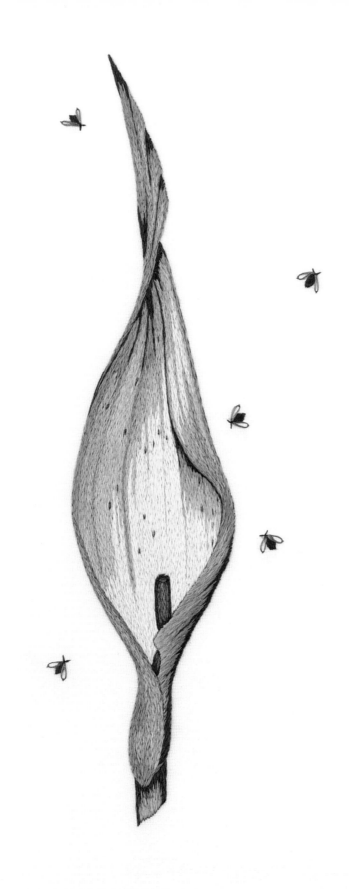

Lords-and-Ladies and Owl Midges

Arum maculatum and *Psychodidae*

LORDS-AND-LADIES

Piercing up through the layers of decomposing leaves lords-and-ladies is one of the first signs of life in the UK's woodlands and shady hedgerows. In early to mid-spring, its arrow-shaped leaves will appear followed by the flower stalk. A large bract leaf, known as the spathe, unfurls like a monk's cowl to reveal a purple-brown central column called the spadix. The small flowers of the plant are found around the lower part of the spadix.

Lords-and-ladies has more folk names than any other British plant. Common names include: cuckoo pint, wake robin, parson-in-the-pulpit, priest's pintle, devils and angels, willy lily, soldier-in-a-sentry-box and jack-in-the-pulpit. Many of the bawdier names are in reference to its sexually evocative shape (there is a suggestion that 'pint', rhyming with 'mint', is short for 'pintel', coming from the old English for penis).

As well as many folk beliefs around the plant, such as placing a leaf in a young man's shoe on the way to a dance to give him the pick of the girls, the roots would also be used as a starch to stiffen lace ruffs in the Elizabethan era.

Perhaps the most fascinating aspect of this plant is the beautiful symbiotic relationship with the owl midge, which has evolved to aid pollination. Not all insects are attracted to the sweet smell of flowers – some prefer a more pungent odour. Lords-and-ladies has evolved to give off a scent like rotting meat, which is enhanced by the increase in temperature within the spathe. To add to the draw of this plant it has developed pollen that will faintly glow at dusk. Irresistibly drawn to the warmth, light and smell, the owl midge will climb down into the lower portion of the plant where it is trapped by slippery walls and downward-pointing hairs. Any pollen already on the midge is transferred and the plant is fertilized. The insect is then treated to nectar and covered in new pollen. The sides of the plant dry and the hairs wither to allow the midge to escape and, not being the smartest of flies, it will continue to the next plant where it will be imprisoned once again.

Following fertilization, the plant will develop bright red and orange berries, which should be avoided as they are poisonous to humans.

OWL MIDGE

It would be very easy to miss the owl midge as it only measures 2–4mm ($^1/_{16}$ – $^3/_{16}$in), but look very closely and you will see one of the cutest, moth-like flies. With a tiny furry body and black-and-white wings covered in grey or light brown hairs, they almost look like an owl when stationary.

The term 'midge' refers to several families of small, gnat-like flies, most of which are completely harmless to humans and will not bite. Sometimes referred to as moth flies, drain flies, filter flies or sewage flies, the owl midge will lay its eggs in stagnant water or hollow rotting trees where the larvae will develop and feed off the slime that can develop in drains and waste pipes. Huge swarms can often be seen around sewage filter beds.

The adults are typically nocturnal but can be seen during daylight hours in shady spots and can be attracted to the light of our windows. This is possibly why lords-and-ladies has developed glowing pollen.

It would be easy to question the purpose of such midges, apart from the pollination of lords-and-ladies, but it is useful to note that as well as the larvae aiding the decomposition process, the adults also provide an excellent food source for bats and other insect-eating predators.

Of course, lords-and-ladies isn't the only plant that is pollinated by midges: without the humble midge we would not have chocolate. The small flowers of the cocoa tree only last for one or two days, and in that time it is really only one pollinator – the ceratopogonid midge – that is small enough to access the hooded, pollen-producing anthers, fertilizing the plant and allowing the cocoa bean to grow.

Threads used

I have used DeVere Yarns threads
for this project (6 thread/120 denier)

FOR THE PLANT

Dark green – DeVere 'Acantus'
Medium green – DeVere 'Ivy'
Green – DeVere 'Verdigrils'
Light green – DeVere 'Basil'
Lightest green – DeVere 'Linden'
Dark brown – DeVere 'Acorn'
Medium brown – DeVere 'All-Spice'
Light brown – DeVere 'Nut'

FOR THE MIDGES

Dark brown – DeVere 'Acorn'
Light brown – DeVere 'Nut'

Template: page 137

Stitches used

Long-and-short stitch (page 32)
Split stitch (page 37)
Satin stitch (page 38)
Lazy-daisy stitch (page 40)

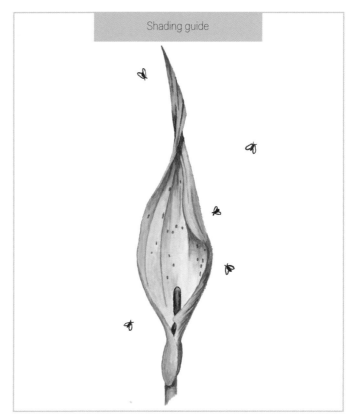

Shading guide

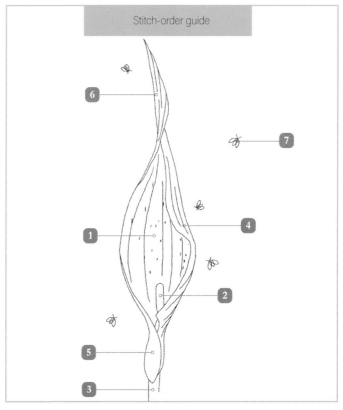

Stitch-order guide

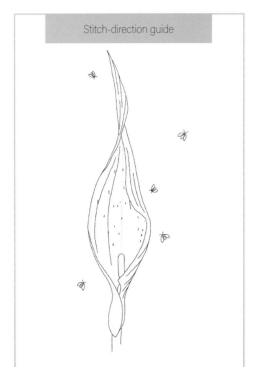

Stitch-direction guide

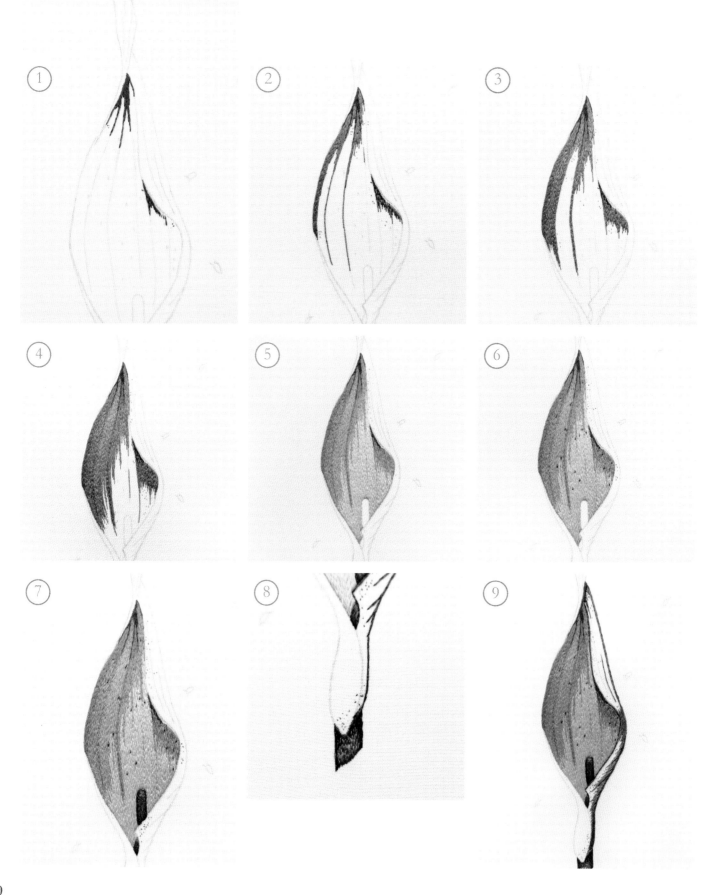

How to stitch

STEP 1: Starting with the central section of the plant, use dark green (Acantus) to start working in long-and-short stitch extending down the veins a little way. Increase the stitches as the veins separate.

STEP 2: Using medium green (Ivy), work around the veins you have already stitched and stretch these further down the plant. The veins will become some of your stitch-direction lines.

STEP 3: Continue shading down the plant in green (Verdigrils) using long-and-short stitch, increasing the stitches as the plant widens.

STEP 4: Continue the shading in light green (Basil). This colour will nearly fill the left-hand side of the plant as the curve places more shade in this area. You will need to decrease the stitches slightly as the plant narrows towards the bottom.

STEP 5: Fill the remaining sections in lightest green (Linden).

STEP 6: Using the original template as a guide, add the brown spots by adding two to three tiny stitches in medium brown (All-Spice) dotted around the central section of the plant.

STEP 7: The spadix is stitched using dark brown (Acorn), medium brown (All-Spice) and light brown (Nut). Work up and down in split stitch, adding the lighter browns running up the centre and curving slightly at the top

STEP 8: The stem of the plant is stitched using dark green (Acantus), medium green (Ivy) and green (Verdigrils). Remember that the plant will create a little shade at the top of the stem and appear lightest in the middle, where the light hits it.

STEP 9: Working next on the outer right-hand side of the plant, use dark green (Acantus) to split stitch the outline and add the first layer of shading in long-and-short stitch. Continue the shading a little using medium green (Ivy). The stitches at the bottom create a down-and-around sweep.

STEP 10: Continue the long-and-short-stitch shading in green (Verdigrils), again using the veins to help with your stitch direction.

STEP 11: Using light green (Basil), continue shading around the fold of the spathe, filling the entire bottom section and most of the top.

STEP 12: Fill the remaining part of the fold of the spathe with lightest green (Linden).

STEP 13: Outline and shade the bottom left-hand section of the plant in medium green (Ivy), allowing the flow of your stitches to follow the shape of the plant.

STEP 14: Continue shading this area in green (Verdigrils).

STEP 15: Fill the remaining part of the bottom left-hand section in light green (Basil).

STEP 16: The top section of the plant (the twist of the spathe) should be outlined in medium green (Ivy). The shading should follow the same pattern as the previous areas, using dark green (Acantus), medium green (Ivy), green (Verdigrils) and light green (Basil) for tonal variation.

STEP 17: The bodies of the midges are stitched using dark brown (Acorn). I have created a very small, pointed area of satin stitch, with two small, straight stitches for the antennae. As there is no area to create a waste knot, when tying off you will need to thread your floss through the stitches on the reverse a couple of times to secure it.

STEP 18: To create the wings, use light brown (Nut) in lazy-daisy stitch. Your starting and finishing point is at the top of the body just below the antennae. Again, you will need to secure your thread through stitches on the reverse as there is no room for a waste knot.

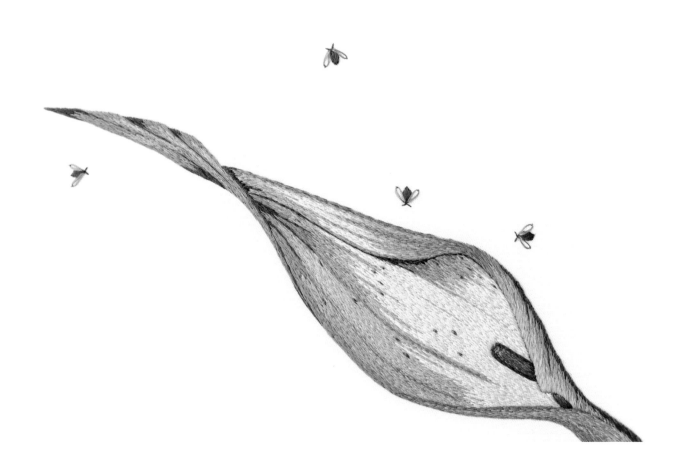

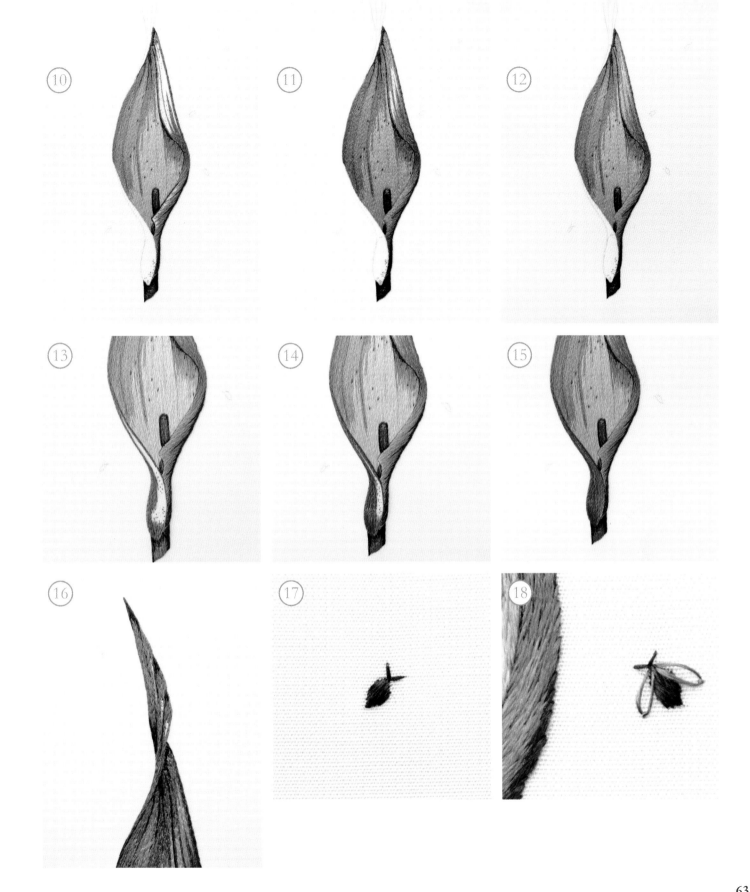

Ox-eye Daisy and Hoverfly

Leucanthemum vulgare and *Syrphus ribesii*

OX-EYE DAISY

Long, hot, summer car journeys are often lifted by the sight of these cheerful large daisies gently dancing by the roadside. One of the first flowers to grow in untreated grassland, it is a welcome sight throughout spring and summer, offering nectar to flies and other essential pollinators.

The large white flowerhead with its yellow disc crammed full of tiny florets was named ox-eye daisy by the ancient Greeks, as it reminded them of the eyes of their oxen. However, the plant has been known by several other common names including moon daisy, moonpenny, dog daisy, horse daisy and marguerite. The reference to the moon derives from the fact that this brilliant white flower almost seems to glow under the moonlight on a midsummer's night.

The ox-eye daisy would often feature in solstice decorations and the flowers used to be hung in cottages to deter fleas. It seems that there are also some culinary uses for the flower: apparently the unopened flowerbuds, when marinated, taste like capers. It is said that cows don't generally like the bitter taste, but if they do eat the plant it can taint their milk, so farmers will try to avoid it. In traditional medicine, the plant has been used to treat many respiratory problems such as whooping cough and asthma. It has been drunk as a tea and salves made of the plant were often used to treat wounds such as ulcers and bruises.

HOVERFLY

During the summer months I will often find that I am being thoroughly investigated by a curious hoverfly – they especially seem to be interested in my washing as I hang it out. Often mistaken for wasps or bees, due to many species having yellow and black stripes, these friendly garden visitors are completely harmless and have no sting, having developed the stripes to deter predators.

There are over 270 different species of hoverfly in the UK alone and they can vary greatly in size and shape from the delicate marmalade hoverfly to the large hornet mimic. Very few hoverflies have common names and are more often referred to by their Latin names; this could go some way to explaining why they are not as popular as butterflies and bees.

As well as being an excellent indicator of biodiversity and environmental change, the hoverfly is truly the gardener's friend. The maggots of some hoverfly species have a voracious appetite for aphids and can devour as many as three to five hundred during the larval stage before turning into adults.

As adults, hoverflies are a common sight during the summer months, flitting from flower to flower collecting nectar and pollen (they are one of the few insects that can digest pollen), providing an essential pollinating service. Unlike butterflies and bees, which have long tongues, the hoverfly has a relatively simple mouth with no tongue and therefore prefers to visit flowers which present easily-accessible nectar, such as Michaelmas daisies, fennel and apple blossom.

Threads used

I have used DeVere Yarns threads for this project (6 thread/120 denier)

FOR THE OX-EYE DAISY

Medium green – DeVere 'Ivy'
Lighter green – DeVere 'Verdigrils'
White – DeVere 'Crystal'
Light grey – DeVere 'Sterling'
Grey – DeVere 'Foil'
Dark orange-brown – DeVere 'Blaze'
Medium orange – DeVere 'Clementine'
Yellow-orange – DeVere 'Carrot'
Medium yellow – DeVere 'Yolk'

FOR THE HOVERFLY

Black – DeVere 'Ebony'
Grey – DeVere 'Foil'
Dark grey – DeVere 'Solder'
Medium yellow – DeVere 'Yolk'
Yellow – DeVere 'Gold'
Dark brown – DeVere 'Cigar'
Medium brown – DeVere 'All-Spice'
Light brown-yellow – DeVere 'Ingot'

Template: page 137

Stitches used

Long-and-short stitch (page 32)
Split stitch (page 37)
Satin stitch (page 38)
French knots (page 39)

Shading guide

Stitch-direction guide

66

Stitch-order guide

How to stitch

STEP 1: Work up and down the stem using split stitch in medium green (Ivy) and lighter green (Verdigrils). Work three rows of medium green to the right of the stem and then fill the remaining area with lighter green.

STEP 2: Outline all the petals in split stitch using white (Crystal). Try to create an understanding of which petals lie behind and which in front. Generally, the petal to the right will lie on top of the petal to the left.

STEP 3: Using grey (Foil), start stitching the darkest areas of each petal in split stitch. In areas where petals lie behind others, try to stitch the areas in the background first.

STEP 4: Following the shading guide, work around the areas of grey using light grey (Sterling). Again, try to remember which petals lie in the background and which in the foreground.

STEP 5: Fill the remaining areas of each petal in white (Crystal), working up and down the petals in split stitch and working background areas before those in the foreground.

STEP 6: Starting with dark orange-brown (Blaze), fill the darkest areas of the disc with French knots, winding your thread around your needle two to three times according to preference. You will need to keep the knots in each colour reasonably close at the bottom and disperse them as you move up.

STEP 7: Working on from the darker knots, and filling some of the gaps within them, continue shading in medium orange (Clementine) French knots. The bottom area of the disc, under the hoverfly and the dimple, will be the darkest areas if the light is coming from directly above.

STEP 8: Continue working your French knots in the disc of the daisy using yellow-orange thread (Carrot). You will need to add occasional knots throughout the rest of the disc to add texture to the final colour.

STEP 9: Fill the remaining area of the disc with medium yellow (Yolk). Make sure that your French knots are close together to give the impression of a tightly packed disc of florets.

STEP 10: Outline the hoverfly in black (Ebony) split stitch and start long-and-short shading the black areas of the hoverfly's abdomen. Use the section lines on the abdomen to guide your stitch direction.

STEP 11: To add the shine, fill in the highlighted areas of the abdomen within the black using grey (Foil).

STEP 12: Fill the bands of the abdomen with medium yellow (Yolk) and yellow (Gold). Lining up the yellow (Gold) with the grey to create a continuation of the highlight.

STEP 13: Using satin stitch, fill the small area of the underside of the thorax with dark brown (Cigar).

STEP 14: The upper side of the thorax should be filled with medium brown (All-Spice) and light brown-yellow (Ingot) for the highlight. Allow some of the black stitches to show to give the impression of sections. The small overlap area onto the abdomen can be filled with light brown-yellow (Ingot).

STEP 15: Using split stitch, work around the eye in yellow (Gold). Do not cover the black outline stitches, as these will give definition against the medium yellow of the flower disc.

STEP 16: Fill in the eye using split stitch in dark brown (Cigar) and medium brown (All-Spice). You can use dark brown (Cigar) to add the antennae leading off from the top of the head and a small stitch for the mouth. Stitch the legs in black (Ebony). You may need to add more than one length of thread for each leg segment to ensure they stand out against the French knots.

STEP 17: Using dark grey (Solder), fill the wings with long stitches. Some stitches will not run the whole length of the wing, to allow you to decrease the number of threads meeting at the point. Add veins of medium brown (All-Spice). The veins will need to cross over some of the dark grey stitches to ensure they do not sink and get lost.

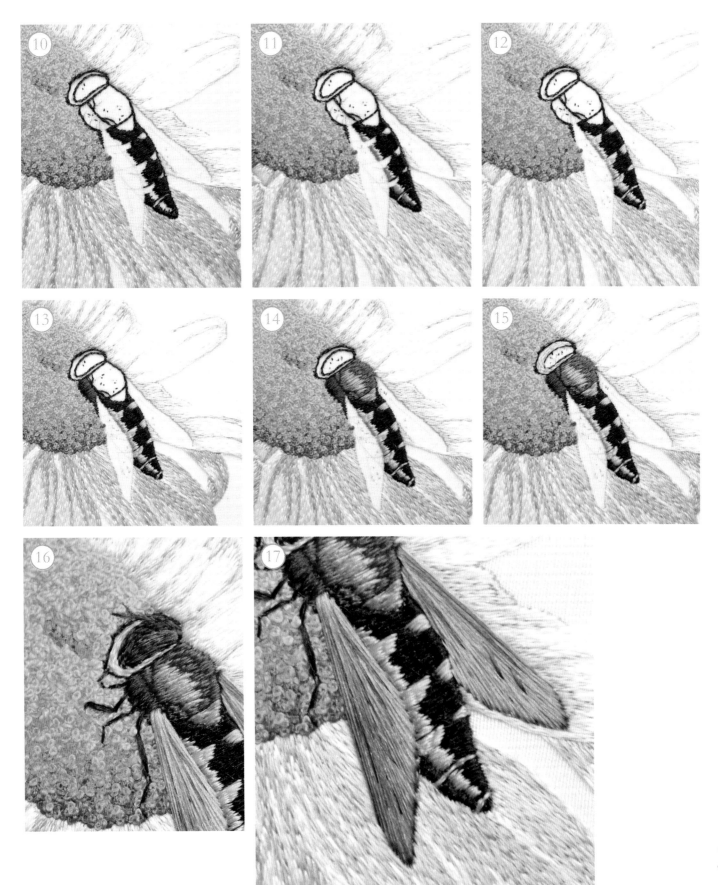

Fennel and Seven-spot Ladybird

Foeniculum vulgare and *Coccinella septempunctata*

FENNEL

Often seen growing along waysides and rough rocky sites, fennel is well known for its culinary and medicinal properties. The large bulbs sold at greengrocers and supermarkets are the cultivated variety Florence Fennel, but the wild plant has the same aniseed flavour and similar culinary uses.

A member of the carrot family, this perennial plant was originally introduced to Britain by the Romans and has since become widely naturalized, working its way into British folklore and medicinal practices. Growing up to 2m (6ft) high with fine feathery leaves and yellow, umbrella-like clusters of flowers, fennel can be seen from midsummer to mid-autumn.

All parts of the fennel plant are edible, however, the stalks can be rather tough so should be cut early in the summer. Parts of the plant can be used freshly cut or hung to dry and stored for winter – in fact, the scent and flavour strengthens as the plant dries. The seeds should be harvested in mid-autumn and can be used as a remedy for trapped wind, coughs and digestive problems. Brightly coloured, sugar-coated fennel seeds called mukhwas are often served in Indian restaurants after a meal to aid digestion and freshen the breath.

Although not originally native to the UK, fennel has still managed to work its way into our folklore. In Somerset, it was pinned over doorways to keep fire from the house and at midsummer it gave protection from enchantment. It is also said that a few fennel seeds in a keyhole will rid your house of ghosts.

Fennel is a wonderful plant to grow in your nature garden – its bright yellow flowerheads are rich in nectar and pollen and will attract an impressive variety of pollinators.

SEVEN-SPOT LADYBIRD

Is there anything as cheerful as a ladybird (known as a ladybug in the US)? Even the collective noun is a 'loveliness', which reflects the affection with which ladybirds are held. Ladybirds have featured in our folklore, children's rhymes and literature for centuries and have been used to predict everything from the weather to suitable marriage partners. It is perhaps no wonder that it has long been considered bad luck to kill or harm one.

The name 'ladybird' dates to the Middle Ages and the cult of the Virgin Mary. The number seven represented the seven joys and seven sorrows and the red was the blood of Christ reflected in the red cloak that Mary was often depicted wearing. The seven-spot ladybird was therefore often seen as a blessing from heaven. While Americans may refer to them as 'ladybugs', in the UK they are known as 'birds', as it was believed they were messengers from heaven and far too graceful to be referred to as 'bugs'.

Their bright colours act as a deterrent to predators and they can also exude a strong-smelling yellow fluid from their leg joints when threatened, which can stain your hands and clothes. In the past, people would sometimes eat ladybirds in the belief that the yellow fluid would act as a cure for toothache.

The seven-spot is one of the most common of our fifty-two species of ladybird and perhaps the most easily recognized due to its representation in art and children's books. They are considered the gardener's friend as both the larvae and adults feed predominantly on aphids – in fact, an adult ladybird can eat up to five thousand aphids during its year-long lifespan.

In the UK, ladybirds now face a threat from the invasion of the non-native harlequin, which sadly has an appetite for eating native UK species. While harlequins are generally larger than the UK's native species, it can be very difficult to differentiate between them and that is why it is best not to try to destroy them in case the identification is wrong. Instead, we should try to help native ladybirds by planting flowers such as yarrow, fennel and tansy, and by leaving log piles and dead flower stems where they can hibernate.

Threads used

I have used DeVere Yarns threads for this project (6 thread/120 denier)

FOR THE LADYBIRD/LADYBUG

Bright red – DeVere 'Glace'
Medium red – DeVere 'Roseate'
Dark red – DeVere 'Grape'
Peach – DeVere 'Sunrise'
Black – DeVere 'Ebony'
White – DeVere 'White'
Medium grey – DeVere 'Solder'
Light grey – DeVere 'Steam'
Dark brown – DeVere 'Acorn'
Medium brown – DeVere 'Nut'

FOR THE FENNEL

Dark yellow – DeVere 'Yolk'
Light yellow – DeVere 'Gold'
Medium green – DeVere 'Ivy'
Light green – DeVere 'Verdigrils'

Template: page 138

Stitches used

Long-and-short stitch (page 32)
Split stitch (page 37)
French knots (page 39)

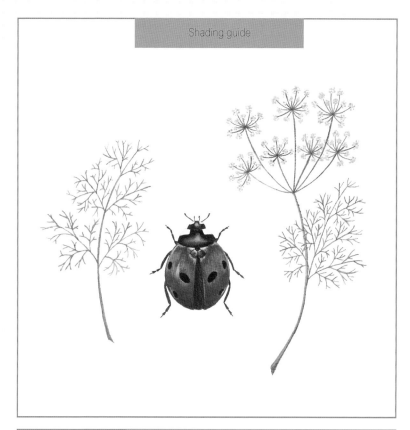

Shading guide

Stitch-direction guide

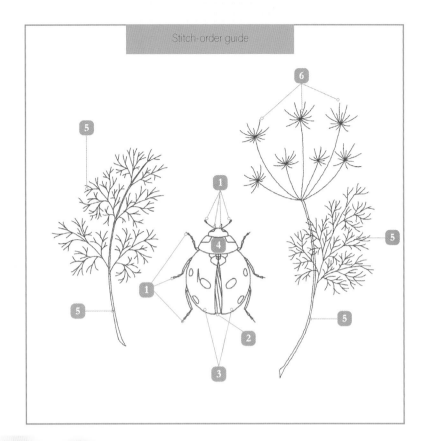

Stitch-order guide

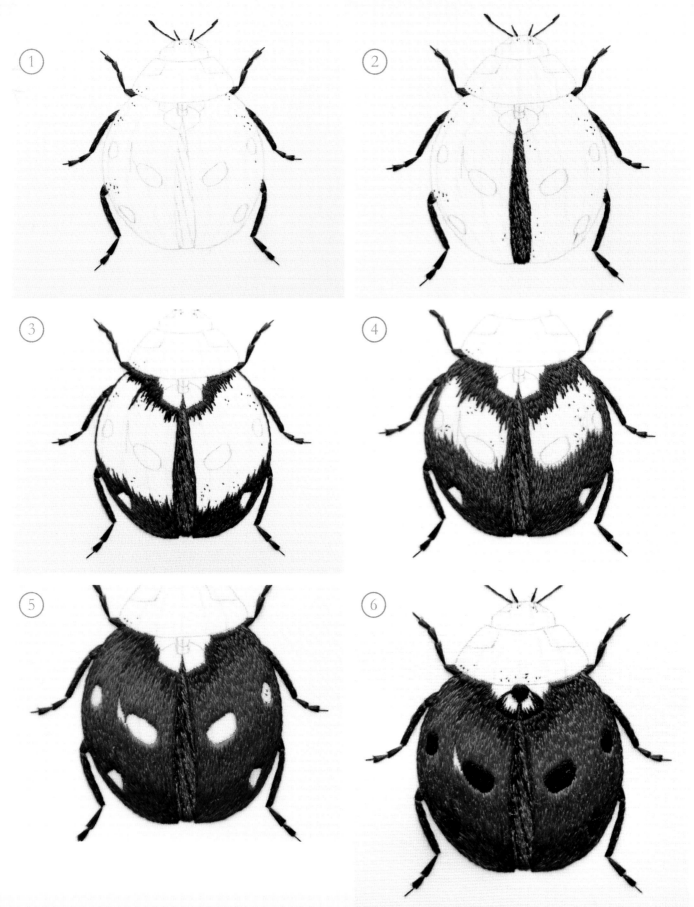

How to stitch

STEP 1: Split stitch all six legs using one line of black (Ebony) on the shaded side and dark brown (Acorn) to fill the upper side. Split stitch the antennae in black, adding an extra stitch at the tips to thicken them.

STEP 2: Fill the area of wing between the wing cases in long-and-short stitch. Stitch the veins and the left-hand side of this area in dark brown (Acorn), then fill the rest of the area in medium brown (Nut).

STEP 3: Split stitch the outline of the wing cases in dark red (Grape) and start the first layer of shading in long-and-short stitch; follow the stitch direction and increase the stitches as needed to create the rounded shape.

STEP 4: Continuing from the dark red shade, add in medium red (Roseate), working up the sides and down from the top, as well as creating a larger area at the bottom of the wing cases.

STEP 5: Fill the remaining red area with bright red (Glace), making sure to leave the small area of shine on the left-hand casing.

STEP 6: Fill in the spots with black (Ebony) long-and-short stitch. For the upper central spot, only fill in the top section and one to two rows around the bottom, as the light will be hitting this area.

STEP 7: The highlights within the red area are added in peach (Sunrise), with a touch of white (White) at the centre top. The shading within the top central spot is finished with light grey (Steam) and white (White).

STEP 8: Following the stitch direction lines, fill the first area of shading within the head sections in black (Ebony) long-and-short stitch. It may help to add shading guidelines.

STEP 9: Fill the area of shine on the head in medium grey (Solder) and light grey (Steam).

STEP 10: The remaining areas of the head are stitched in white (White) using long-and-short stitch.

STEP 11: Using medium green (Ivy) and light green (Verdigrils), split stitch the stems and feathered leaves of the fennel. I have used medium green to the right of both stems and light green to the left and for the leaves.

STEP 12: The flowerheads are sewn by stitching small clusters of French knots in dark yellow (Yolk) and light yellow (Gold). I have wound the floss around the needle three times to make the knots large enough.

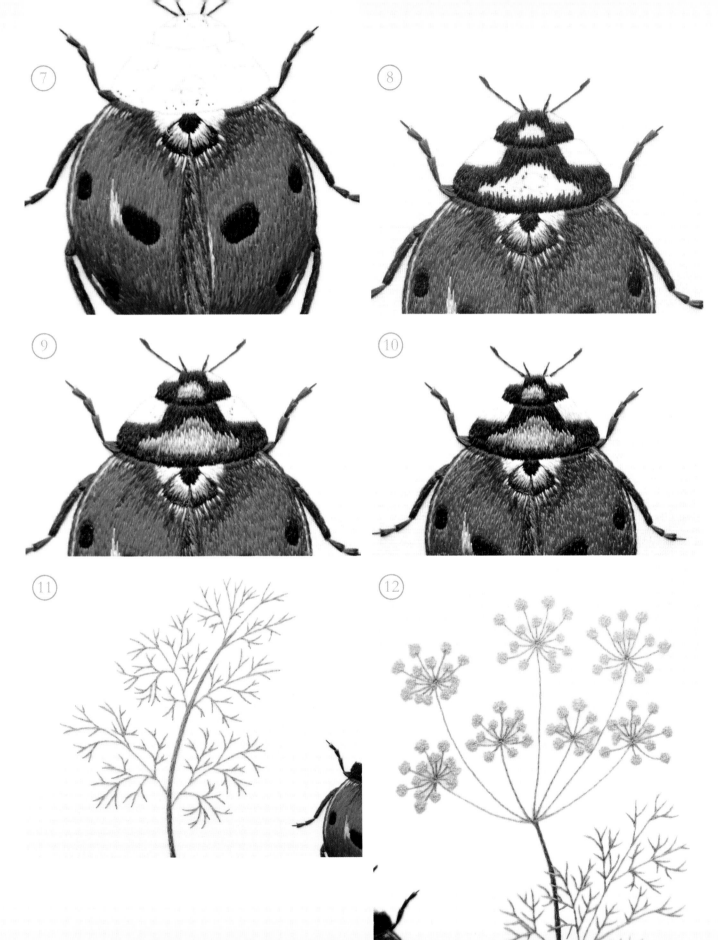

7

8

9

10

11

12

79

Meadow Buttercup and Thick-legged Flower Beetle

Ranunculus acris and *Oedemera nobilis*

MEADOW BUTTERCUP

'Do you like butter?' is a question you will often hear children ask during the summer months as they hold a buttercup under their friend's chin. If the sun is shining, the flower will reflect a beautiful yellow glow, proving that the answer to the question is indeed 'yes'. I would be lying if I said that I have never done this as an adult – the bright yellow glow in a spring meadow is just too tempting.

The tall and stately meadow buttercup flowers from late spring into late summer and usually prefers damp calcareous (chalky) soil. It is one of the first flowers to turn a spring meadow yellow, much to the distress of farmers, as cattle can be poisoned by eating too many of them. Luckily the plant has a rather acrid taste and this seems to be enough of a deterrent to farm animals as cases of serious poisoning seem to be few. Despite the plant's reputation for causing irritation, it would often be included in May Day garlands to celebrate the end of winter and to welcome the warmer days ahead.

While the name 'buttercup' seems an obvious choice given the dairy-like colour, it didn't actually come into general use until the eighteenth century. Before this the plant had several common names including: goldweed, soldier buttons and kingcup. Most of these names have now been forgotten, or applied to other wildflowers, but crowpeckle is still used in some areas.

The buttercup is highly visible to pollinators, attracting various short-tongued insects including honey bees, butterflies and thick-legged flower beetles. It achieves its almost mirror-like yellow shine by trapping a thin layer of air between two layers of cells in the petals.

THICK-LEGGED FLOWER BEETLE

On a beautiful summer's day, you may be lucky enough to spot this beautiful beetle shining like a gem as the sun reflects off its metallic green body. The first time I saw one I was fascinated by its colour and, what can only be described as, its rather shapely thighs. The male thick-legged flower beetle is easily identified by its curvaceous, swollen hind 'thighs', which give it the appearance of having worked out at the gym a little too often. The female of the species, on the other hand, has rather skinny-looking legs in comparison.

Also known as swollen-thighed beetles or false oil beetles, these stunning insects can be seen on hot days during spring and summer feeding on pollen and nectar from open-structured flowers such as ox-eye daisies, buttercups and bramble flowers.

Adult thick-legged flower beetles can be easily spotted with their long, thin elytra (the hardened forewings that protect the hind-wings underneath), which don't quite meet at the base, leaving the underwings exposed. However, it can be near impossible to spot the larvae, which will remain well-concealed in the dry stems of plants such as thistle, where they will feed and grow before emerging as adults.

The thick-legged flower beetle is part of the false blister beetle family (*Oedemeridae*), so named due to their resemblance to true 'blister beetles'. Many of these insects contain a blistering chemical called cantharidin, which serves as a deterrent to predators. Cantharidin has traditionally been used in the treatment of warts and, rather worryingly, as an aphrodisiac.

Threads used

I have used Pipers Silks floss silks for this project

FOR THE BUTTERCUP

Light yellow – Pipers 'Jasmine'
Medium yellow – Pipers 'King Cup'
Dark yellow – Pipers 'Saffron Brown'
Light green – Pipers 'Fir Green'
Medium green – Pipers 'Leaf'
Dark green – Pipers 'Forest Green'
Dark green-blue – Pipers 'Tartan'

FOR THE BEETLE

White – Pipers 'White'
Black – Pipers 'Black'
Brown – Pipers 'Brown'
Light brown – Pipers 'Pine'
Dark green-blue – Pipers 'Tartan'
Green-blue – Pipers 'Green Blue'
Light green-blue – Pipers 'Pastel Green'
Yellow-green – Pipers 'Moss'

Template: page 139

Stitches used

Long-and-short stitch (page 32)
Split stitch (page 37)
Satin stitch (page 38)
French knots (page 39)

Shading guide	Stitch-direction guide

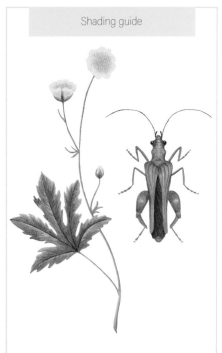
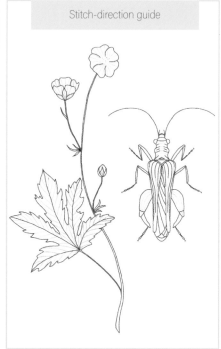

Stitch-order guide

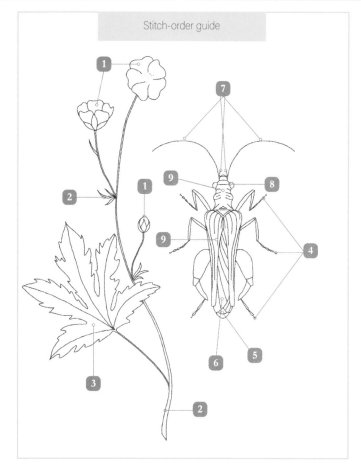

How to stitch

STEP 1: Following the stitch-direction guide, sew the two buttercups and bud in long-and-short stitch using light yellow (Jasmine), medium yellow (King Cup) and dark yellow (Saffron Brown). Shade the colours from light to dark, working towards the centre of the flower (1a and 1b).

STEP 2: Using dark yellow (Saffron Brown) and light yellow (Jasmine), fill the centre of both buttercups with scattered French knots, winding the thread around your needle two or three times according to preference.

STEP 3: Use long-and-short stitch to fill the sepals of the flowers and the bud in light green (Fir Green) to medium green (Leaf). Work from light to dark towards the base of each sepal.

STEP 4: Using light green (Fir Green) and medium green (Leaf), split stitch the stalk and small leaves. I have used two lines of medium green to the right of the stalk and filled the remaining area with light green. The underside of the small leaves is shaded with medium green.

STEP 5: Split stitch the outline of the main leaf in medium green (Leaf).

STEP 6: Following the shading guide and stitch-direction guide, sew the five lobes with long-and-short stitch using light green (Fir Green), medium green (Leaf) and dark green (Forest Green). Increase and decrease your stitches as necessary where each segment joins the next.

STEP 7: Using your dark green-blue (Tartan), split stitch the veins down the centre of each leaf segment and stretching out at even intervals.

STEP 8: Using dark green-blue (Tartan), green-blue (Green Blue) and light green-blue (Pastel Green), stitch the flower beetle's legs. The darker colours will be on the bottom side of the legs. The thin legs are formed using split stitch for the first two sections and with single stitches forming a triangle for the remaining smaller segments. The thick legs are sewn in long-and-short stitch following the guidelines and adding yellow-green (Moss) as the highlight.

STEP 9: Stitch the small area of abdomen visible behind the wings in dark green-blue (Tartan) and green-blue (Green Blue), using split stitch and the curved line as shown in the template (which should be sewn in dark green-blue) to guide your stitches.

STEP 10: The wings are stitched in long-and-short stitch using brown (Brown) and light brown (Pine). The veins of the wings are sewn in brown and the shading is a continuation of this, as shown in the shading guide (and photograph on pages 88–89).

STEP 11: Using black (Black), sew the antennae in split stitch and the eyes in small areas of satin stitch. Add a couple of stitches of white (White) to the eyes to add highlights.

STEP 12: Outline the head and body in dark green-blue (Tartan) and add the first layer of shading. Follow the shading guide to understand where the darkest areas lie.

STEP 13: Continue the shading, following on from your darkest colour, in green-blue (Green Blue).

STEP 14: Using light green-blue (Pastel Green), follow on your shading – this layer will nearly fill the whole beetle.

STEP 15: Fill the remaining areas with yellow-green (Moss) – this will create the highlights and really make the beetle shine.

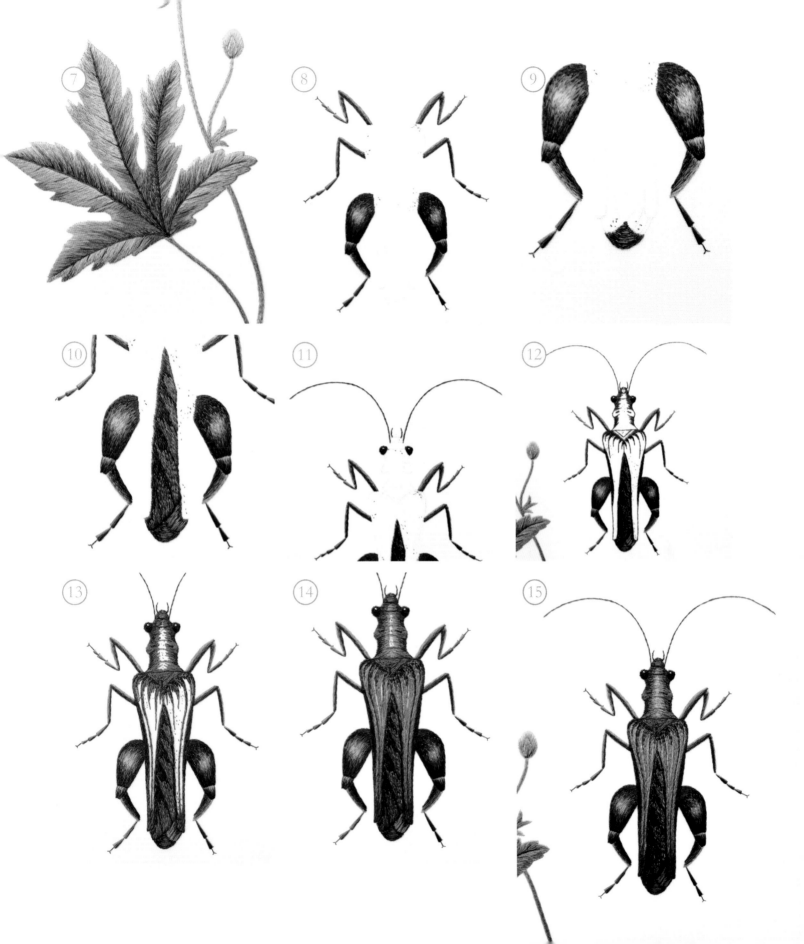

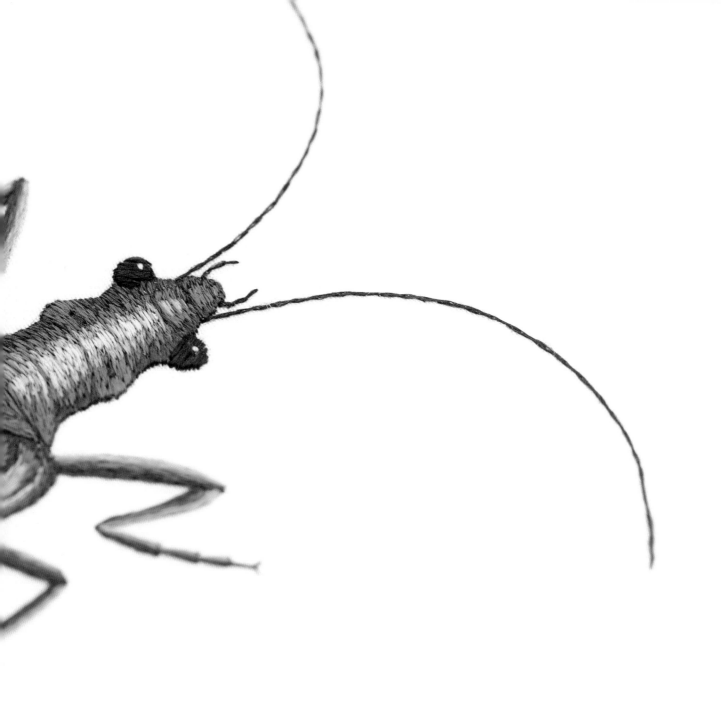

Bramble and Gatekeeper Butterfly

Rubus fruticosus and *Pyronia tithonus*

BRAMBLE

For so many of us late summer brings memories of blackberry picking, scratching our arms and staining our fingers in an attempt to reconnect with nature and forage for our food. Coming home with a bowl full of blackberries and turning them into jellies, cordials and crumbles is a seasonal treat, but do be sure not to pick them by railways or busy roads. With over 400 microspecies of bramble it is no wonder that the taste can vary so much, from mouth-puckering sharpness to a delicate sweet flavour that leaves you wanting to eat most of your harvest before you get home. The tradition of blackberry picking has been found to go back thousands of years, as seeds have been found in the stomach of a Neolithic man discovered in Essex, UK.

Often found in woodlands and hedgerows, the bramble is a scrambling shrub with long, arching, thorny stems that can root down at the tip and form dense tangles, which provide excellent protection for nesting birds. Flowering from late spring, its pretty white and pink petals attract many pollinating insects and provide an excellent source of nectar; then in late summer the blackberries help many of our birds and mammals to feed up in preparation for winter.

There are many folklores surrounding the bramble, from passing a child with whooping cough through a bramble shoot that has rooted naturally at either end, to planting it on graves to keep the dead in and the Devil out. It was also said that Satan landed in a bramble patch when he fell from heaven, which is probably why it is said that you should not pick blackberries after Michaelmas day (29th September), as that is when the Devil spits on them.

GATEKEEPER BUTTERFLY

The gatekeeper may not be the largest or the most colourful of butterflies, but the sight of it dancing from flower to flower, patrolling hedges and gateways along country lanes is a welcome sight in midsummer. Preferring warm weather, the gatekeeper butterfly is one of the last to emerge and can be seen seeking out nectar from flowers such as ragwort, thistles and bramble blossoms.

Also known as the hedge brown, small meadow brown and the hedge eye, the gatekeeper butterfly can often be found basking in the sun in hedgerows near long grass on which the female will lay her eggs. Each egg will take about two to three weeks to pupate, after which the caterpillar will feed on the grasses. From early autumn the caterpillars will hibernate, becoming active again the following spring. By late spring or early summer they will be fully grown and will pupate to become adult butterflies.

The eyespots on the forewings of the gatekeeper butterfly act as a deterrent to predators such as birds, and the colour and pattern of the wings can change subtly due to a variety of reasons including temperature change.

Butterflies and moths are very sensitive to habitat change and can be a good indicator of environmental health. Overall, butterfly numbers have decreased by 76 per cent in the UK since 1976. Habitat loss is largely responsible for the decline in site-specific butterflies and, while the long hot summers of recent years have proved beneficial to some, climate change is having a detrimental effect on many species such as the gatekeeper when drought-like conditions dry out important larvae food like grasses.

Threads used

I have used DeVere Yarns threads for this project (6 thread/120 denier)

FOR THE BUTTERFLY

Dark brown – DeVere 'Acorn'
Medium brown – DeVere 'Nut'
Light brown-yellow – DeVere 'Ingot'
Medium grey – DeVere 'Solder'
Orange-brown – DeVere 'Blaze'
Dark orange – DeVere 'Vermillion'
Orange – DeVere 'Clementine'
Orange-yellow – DeVere 'Carrot'
Black – DeVere 'Ebony'
White – DeVere 'White'

FOR THE BRAMBLE

Dark brown – DeVere 'Acorn'
Medium brown – DeVere 'Nut'
Dark green – DeVere 'Ivy'
Light green – DeVere 'Verdigrils'
Pink – DeVere 'Blossom'
Peach – DeVere 'Sunrise'
Cream – DeVere 'Petal'
Pastel yellow – DeVere 'Beeswax'
Dark red – DeVere 'Grape'
White – DeVere 'White'
Black – DeVere 'Ebony'

Template: page 140

Stitches used

Long-and-short stitch (page 32)
Split stitch (page 37)
Satin stitch (page 38)
Seed stitch (page 40)

Shading guide

Stitch-direction guide

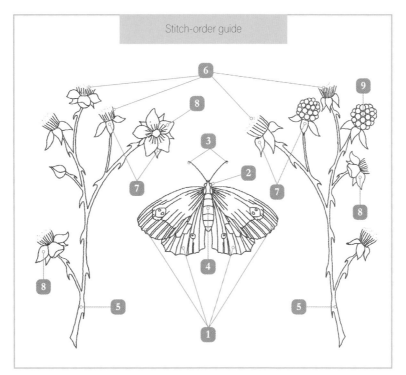

Stitch-order guide

1

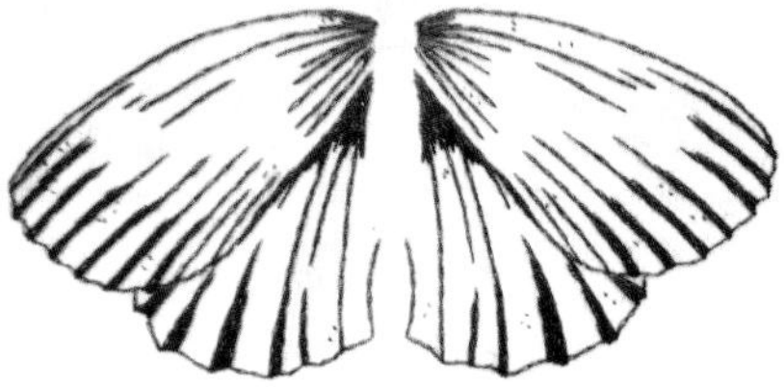

2

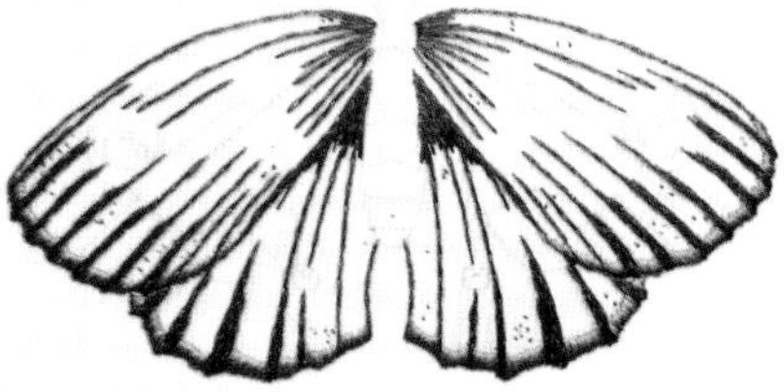

3

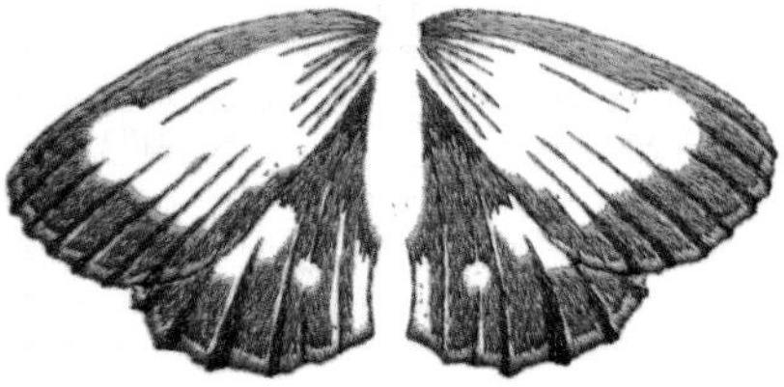

4

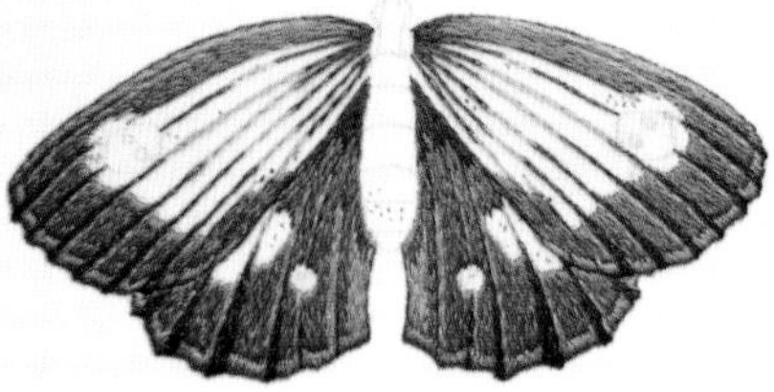

5

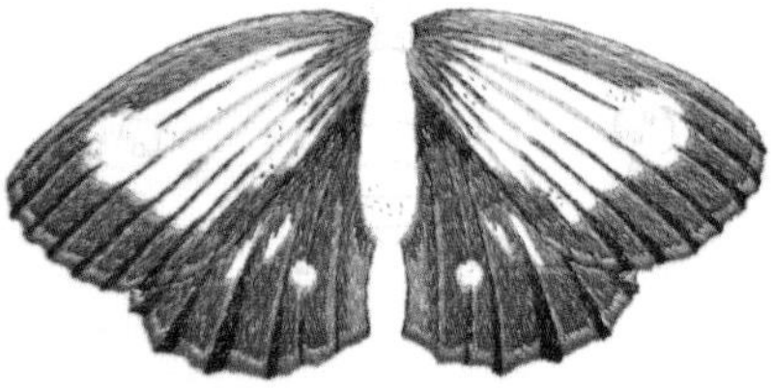

6

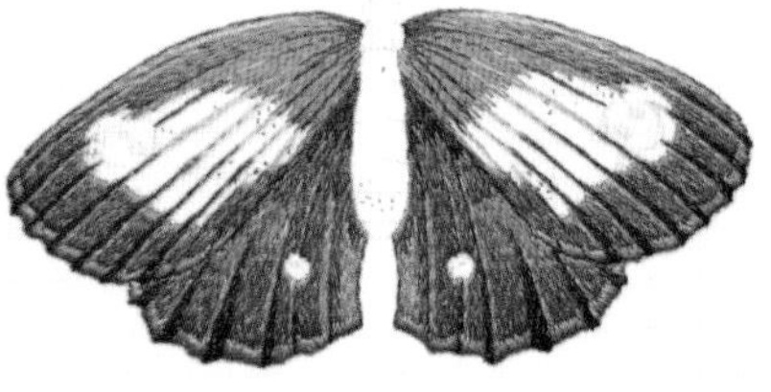

7

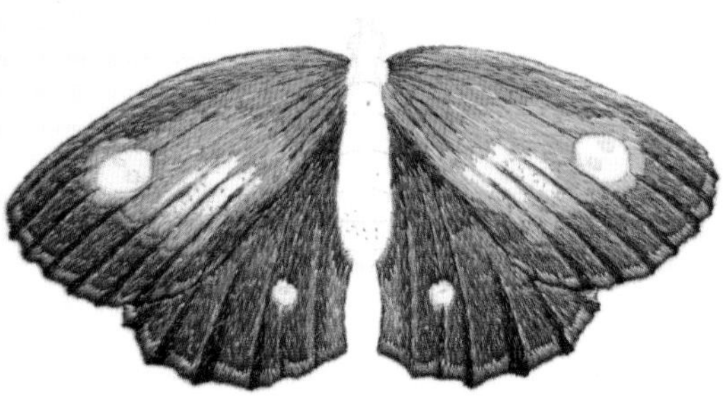

8

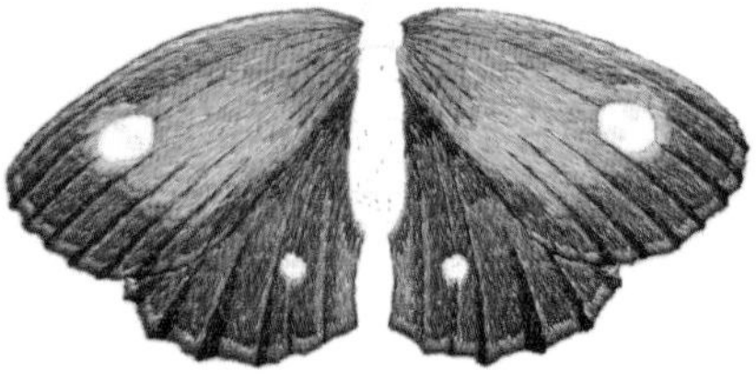

9

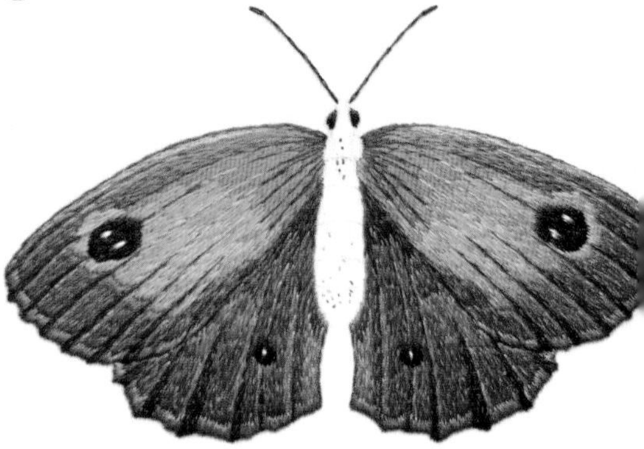

How to stitch

STEP 1: Outline the wings in split stitch using dark brown (Acorn). Stitch the vein lines and, using these to guide your stitch direction, start shading the darkest areas of the wings using long-and-short stitch.

STEP 2: Using medium grey (Solder), add small stitches along the edges of the wings. These will not vary much in length as the line should have a reasonably sharp edge.

STEP 3: Continue the long-and-short stitch shading around the dark brown in medium brown (Nut). Do not finish the vein lines at this point.

STEP 4: Fill in the remaining areas of brown with light brown-yellow (Ingot) and connect up the vein lines.

STEP 5: Using orange-brown (Blaze), shade the darkest orange areas of the wings. This will only be a small area at the top of the upper wings and the darker areas of the lower spots.

STEP 6: Continue long-and-short stitch shading in dark orange (Vermillion), to fill the orange area on the lower wings and most of the top section of the upper wings.

STEP 7: Apart from the black spots and a small area on each upper wing, continue stitching in orange (Clementine).

STEP 8: Fill the remaining areas on the upper wings (apart from the spots) with orange-yellow (Carrot).

STEP 9: Using black (Ebony), fill in the spots on the upper and lower wings using long-and-short stitch. Add one stitch of white (White) to the spots on the lower wings and two sets of three stitches to the spots on the upper wing; try to cross the black stitches so the white doesn't sink in. Satin stitch the eyes and split stitch the antennae in black, adding an extra stitch at the end of each antenna to create a thickness.

STEP 10: Start shading each section on the body in dark brown (Acorn) and continue the shading in medium brown (Nut), using long-and-short stitch (see the photograph on pages 98–99).

STEP 11: I have placed the light source at the centre top so this is reflected in the shading on the bramble branches; shade the darkest side of the branches in rows of split stitch using dark brown (Acorn) and the lighter side in medium brown (Nut).

STEP 12: The filaments of each flower are stitched using single long stitches of slightly varying lengths overlaying each other in light green (Verdigrils), peach (Sunrise) and cream (Petal). Add seed stitches in medium brown (Nut) to the top of the filaments.

STEP 13: Following the stitch-direction lines, sew the bud and sepals in long-and-short stitch using light green (Verdigrils) and dark green (Ivy).

STEP 14: The petals of the flowers are stitched in long-and-short stitch using cream (Petal) and pink (Blossom). The petal turn-overs are also sewn in pink.

STEP 15: The centre of the open flower should be filled with seed stitches in light green (Verdigrils) and pastel yellow (Beeswax); it can become quite difficult to push the needle through when the stitches have built up so you may need your thimble here. The filaments are added on top of the shading in white (White) and finished with a seed stitch going across the shading stitches in medium brown (Nut).

STEP 16: Each drupelet (seed) on the blackberry is sewn using small satin stitches in black (Ebony), with two or three in dark red (Grape). Try to make the direction of your stitches vary from drupelet to drupelet.

STEP 17: Add small seed stitches in cream (Petal) in between each drupelet. At this point you will have no room for waste knots so you will need to thread your floss through the stitches on the reverse.

Common Knapweed and Six-spot Burnet Moth

Centaurea nigra and *Zygaena filipendulae*

COMMON KNAPWEED

Bright pink flowerheads dancing in the breeze are a common sight in summer across UK meadows, verges and grasslands. One of the toughest meadow plants, knapweed is an excellent source of good-quality nectar for many pollinating insects and especially loved by the six-spot burnet moth. The hardy and fast spreading nature of the plant has led it to be considered an invasive species in North America.

Common names for the knapweed include hardheads, paintbrushes, bachelor's buttons and iron knobs, mostly in reference to its thistle-like black/brown flowerheads. Flowers appear in summer, turning to seedheads in late summer and providing a tasty treat for many birds.

In days gone by, knapweed was often used by young women in a love-divination game. The flower would be picked, and the rays pulled out, then the plucked flower would be placed in the lady's blouse waiting for the other unopened flowerheads to bloom. When the flowers opened it would be a sign that her true love was near.

Knapweed flowers are edible and can be added to salads, although the bracts are a little too tough to eat. In the fourteenth century, the flower would be eaten with pepper before a meal to restore a lost appetite and the plant was used in medicine to treat wounds, bruises, scabs and sore throats amongst many other ailments. Modern herbalists prefer to use knapweed as a tonic, a diuretic and to induce sweating.

SIX-SPOT BURNET MOTH

In the middle of a bright summer's day you might catch a glimpse of a black and red insect fluttering from flower to flower. You would be forgiven for thinking it was a butterfly – even early entomologists were unsure and believed them to be halfway between the two. But that insect is likely to be the six-spot burnet, a day-flying moth with forewings that are glossy black with six distinctive red spots, and hindwings of carmine-red with a black edge.

The red spots on the forewings warn predators that the burnet moth is poisonous, releasing hydrogen cyanide when attacked. The yellow-green caterpillar of the burnet moth is also poisonous to predators due to its ability to metabolize toxins contained within its main plant food, bird's foot trefoil. Another defence mechanism used by the burnet moth is to feign death if disturbed and knocked off a plant.

'Burnet moth' is believed to be an old folk name related to the word 'brunette', due to the moth's dark colour, although another more sinister common name is bloodsucker, due to the deep red of the spots and hindwings.

Although it has long been understood that moths help to pollinate night-blooming plants, new research suggests that the role of moths in pollination is far more prolific than first presumed. While bees, hoverflies and butterflies will tend to visit a narrow group of flowers, it has been found that moths are generalists, visiting a wide range of plants, transferring pollen collected on their hairy bodies. Moth numbers have declined rapidly since the 1970s due to habitat loss and the increased use of pesticides. This decline will have an impact on other creatures that rely on moths as a food source, such as bats. So, while it is easy to dismiss moths as dull insects that can destroy your clothes, we really do need to change our perception and start respecting their role in our eco-system.

Threads used

I have used Pipers Silks floss silks for this project

FOR THE KNAPWEED

Pink-purple – Pipers 'Bright Fuchsia'
Muted pink – Pipers 'Orchid Pink'
Pastel pink – Pipers 'Bright Heather'
Brown – Pipers 'Brown'
Dark olive green – Pipers 'Mid Olive'
Dark green – Pipers 'Green'
Medium green – Pipers 'Leaf'
Light green – Pipers 'Pale Leaf'
Light yellow-green – Pipers 'Sycamore'

FOR THE BURNET MOTH

Black – Pipers 'Black'
White – Pipers 'White'
Dark blue-grey – Pipers 'Deep Slate'
Medium grey – Pipers 'Dark Pewter'
Dark red – Pipers 'Kenya Red'
Red – Pipers 'Red'

Template: page 141

Stitches used

Long-and-short stitch (page 32)
Split stitch (page 37)
Satin stitch (page 38)

Shading guide

Stitch-direction guide

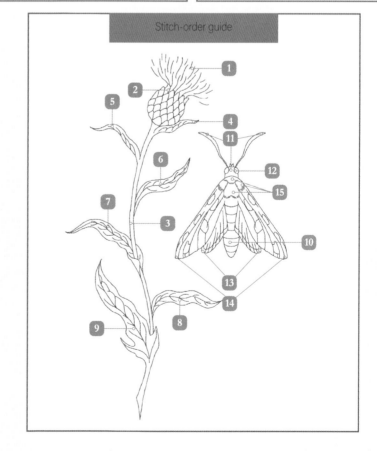

Stitch-order guide

How to stitch

STEP 1: Start by sewing the longest parts of the flower in pink-purple (Bright Fuchsia) using split stitch; these are the lines drawn on the template.

STEP 2: Using muted pink (Orchid Pink), add random stitches in between the pink-purple, as shown. These can be single stitches or smaller split stitches if you prefer. Repeat a second row of similar stitches below that, and then a third row of longer lines in split stitch leading to the bottom of the flowerhead.

STEP 3: Repeat the previous step, filling the remaining areas in using a mix of pinks including pastel pink (Bright Heather).

STEP 4: Each diamond section of the base of the flower is sewn by starting with brown (Brown) stitches of varying lengths fanning out around the top. Next, fill the remaining area of each section with dark olive green (Mid Olive). Each row of diamonds should be completed before starting the next, to give the appearance of overlapping; you may wish to have two needles parked and ready to go.

STEP 5: I have stitched the stem of the plant before the leaves, however, the section of leaf three that lies behind can be stitched first if you prefer. To create the ridges on the stem I have worked lines of split stich up and down from right to left: two lines of dark green (Green), two lines of light green (Pale Leaf), two lines of medium green (Leaf), two lines of light green, one line of medium green and one line of light green. The lines can be increased and decreased at the top and bottom.

STEP 6: Leaf one lies slightly in front of the flowerhead and stem but only shows the underside, which is lighter than the upper side. Add stitch-direction lines, then outline in light green (Pale Leaf) split stitch.

STEP 7: Shade the leaf in long-and-short stitch following the direction lines using light green (Pale Leaf) at the top and medium green (Leaf) at the bottom.

STEP 8: Add the veins of the leaf in light green-yellow (Sycamore) – split stitch over the top of the previous stitches.

STEP 9: Leaf two also shows the underside, so the shading will follow the same pattern as steps 6, 7 and 8.

STEP 10: Leaf three shows the upper side so will be slightly darker than the previous two leaves. I have used, working from the outside of the leaf to the centre, medium green (Leaf) to dark green (Green) on the top half, and dark green to medium green on the bottom. The veins have been stitched in light green (Pale Leaf).

STEP 11: Leaf four shows the upper side of the leaf but has a glimpse of the underside in the turn-over, which will be lighter. The upper side of the leaf is stitched using medium green (Leaf) to dark green (Green) on the top half, and dark green to medium green on the lower section. The turn-over is sewn in satin stitch using light green (Pale Leaf) and the veins are also stitched in this shade.

STEP 12: Leaf five shows the upper side and will follow the same shading as leaf three in step 10.

STEP 13: The final leaf is showing the underside so will be lighter. The shading will follow the pattern of light green (Pale Leaf) to medium green (Leaf) on the right-hand side and medium green to light green on the left. The veins are sewn in light green-yellow (Sycamore). As this leaf is larger than the others, you will need to do more than one row of stitches in each shade in some areas.

STEP 14: Starting with the abdomen of the moth, stitch each section working from black (Black) down to dark blue-grey (Deep Slate), down to medium grey (Dark Pewter). To create the impression of hairs I have slipped the threads in between the stitches of the previous row rather than splitting them.

STEP 15: The head of the moth is filled with long-and-short stitch using black (Black) and dark blue-grey (Deep Slate). The antennae are also stitched in black and dark blue-grey; to create the stripes I have alternated two stitches of each colour – you may wish to have two needles threaded and parked.

STEP 16: Split stitch the outline of the eyes in black (Black) and then cover with satin stitch. Add two tiny stitches of white (White) to each eye to create the shine; the stitches will need to cross over the black to avoid them sinking.

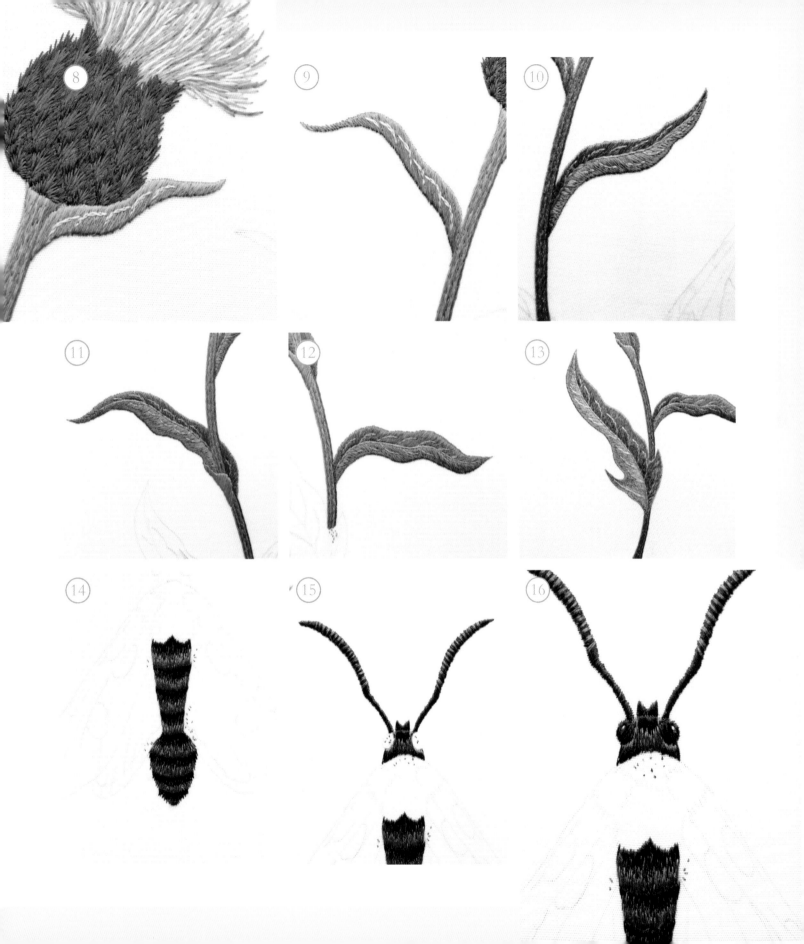

STEP 17: Starting on the hindwings, split stitch the outline and the veins in black (Black). Using single stitches, sew the first line of shading alternating black and dark blue-grey (Deep Slate) following the shading guide. I have not varied the lengths of the stitches as I want this row of colour to have a relatively sharp edge.

STEP 18: Using red (Red) and dark red (Kenya Red), shade in between the veins in long-and-short stitch. The dark red is used at the top of the wing and next to the vein corresponding with the black stitches in the previous step.

STEP 19: Using black (Black), split stitch the outline of the forewings and the veins. Start adding areas of shading in black next to the veins as shown in the shading guide.

STEP 20: Follow on from the areas of black by shading in dark blue-grey (Deep Slate).

STEP 21: Fill the remaining dark sections of the forewings with medium grey (Dark Pewter).

STEP 22: Fill the spots with dark red (Kenya Red) and red (Red), roughly matching the areas of dark red with the dark grey.

STEP 23: I have separated the thorax of the moth into four sections. Starting with the side sections, shade with black (Black) around the edges and dark blue-grey (Deep Slate) in the centre. Add your direction lines if it helps.

STEP 24: The central lower section is shaded in black (Black) around the edges to dark blue-grey (Deep Slate), and then to medium grey (Dark Pewter).

STEP 25: Fill the remaining area of the thorax with black (Black) stitches to finish.

Blackthorn and Buff-tailed Bumblebee

Prunus spinosa and *Bombus terrestris*

BLACKTHORN

A profusion of white blossom fills our woodlands, scrub and hedgerows in spring as the blackthorn bursts into life before many other plants, offering an early feast of nectar for insects just emerging from hibernation. This deciduous shrub can grow up to 4m (13ft) or more tall, makes an excellent hedging plant and, with its very hard wood and long thorns, offers a safe refuge for nesting birds, protecting them from predators. Not only does the blackthorn provide leaves as food for many moth and butterfly caterpillars, it also feeds birds in autumn with its small acidic plums known as sloes.

Given the strength of its wood, blackthorn was often used to make walking sticks and, in Devon, UK, it was believed that witches carrying a stick made of the wood could cause all sorts of mischief. The plant is surrounded in folklore, mostly involving witches using the thorns for various spells, but the blackthorn is also linked to Christianity, as it is one of the plants reputed to have formed the thorny crown of Christ at the crucifixion. A spell of cold weather in spring is often referred to as a 'blackthorn winter', as the white blossom reflects the snow in the adjacent fields.

While all cultivated plums are descendants of the blackthorn, the sloe berry is far too tart to be eaten as it is. Perhaps its best use is in sloe gin – ideally the berries should be picked after the first frost in early to mid-autumn (or a spell in your freezer is a good alternative). The sloes should be pricked with a skewer and a jar half-filled with the berries and half their weight in sugar. Fill the jar with gin and store for at least two months, giving it an occasional shake. The drink should be ready just in time for Christmas.

BUFF-TAILED BUMBLEBEE

In early spring you will often hear a gentle tapping at your window as a queen buff-tailed bumblebee searches the garden for her first feed of nectar after waking from hibernation. She will need to replenish her food reserves before searching for a nest site, which will usually be found in an old mouse hole. Her nest will eventually contain anything from one hundred to six hundred bees so she will need all the energy she can get. Winter planting for pollinators is crucial to help these early visitors.

Only the queen bumblebee has a buff-coloured tail; worker bees are smaller and have white hairs on their bottom. The female bees will store pollen in baskets on their hind legs and their short tongues will sometimes lead them to become 'nectar robbers' – they will bite a small hole in the base of a flower that is too deep for them to access, allowing them to suck the nectar out.

Sometimes referred to as dumbledores, dusty millers and bummie-bees, the name bumblebee only came into common use in the twentieth century – before this they were known as humble bees. The name did not suggest that they are humble in any way but rather it referred to the gentle hum they make as they fly.

There are 24 species of bumblebee within the UK with two species sadly now extinct (there are around 250 species worldwide). The decline in bumblebee numbers is of great concern; seven bumblebee species have declined by more than 50 per cent in the last 25 years. This decline can mostly be attributed to habitat loss, as 97 per cent of flower-rich meadows have been lost since 1937. Bumblebees are great pollinators and play a key role in pollinating much of the food we eat as well as our native wildflowers. Their decline could have a major impact on the countryside as we know it, so it is important that we keep bumblebees in mind when planting our pollinator gardens.

Threads used

I have used Pipers Silks floss silks for this project

FOR THE BUMBLEBEE

Black – Pipers 'Black'
White – Pipers 'White'
Grey – Pipers 'Grey'
Dark yellow – Pipers 'Kingcup'
Light yellow – Pipers 'Light Gold'
Beige – Pipers 'Pale Mushroom'
Cream – Pipers 'Mid Ecru'
Light brown – Pipers 'Pine'
Dark brown – Pipers 'Brown'
Orange – Pipers 'Marigold'

FOR THE BLACKTHORN

Black – Pipers 'Black'
White – Pipers 'White'
Dark brown – Pipers 'Brown'
Light brown – Pipers 'Pine'
Beige – Pipers 'Pale Mushroom'
Blue-grey – Pipers 'Lavender'
Dark green – Pipers 'Mermaid'
Medium green – Pipers 'Forest Green'
Light green – Pipers 'Fir Green'
Light yellow – Pipers 'Light Gold'
Dark blue-purple – Pipers 'Viola'
Light blue-purple – Pipers 'Medium Pansy'

Template: page 142

Stitches used

Long-and-short stitch (page 32)
Split stitch (page 37)
French knots (page 39)
Satin stitch (page 38)

Shading guide

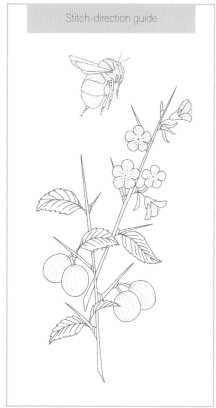

Stitch-direction guide

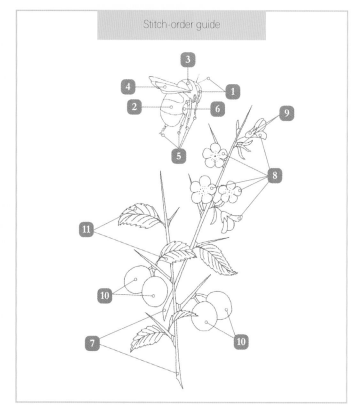

Stitch-order guide

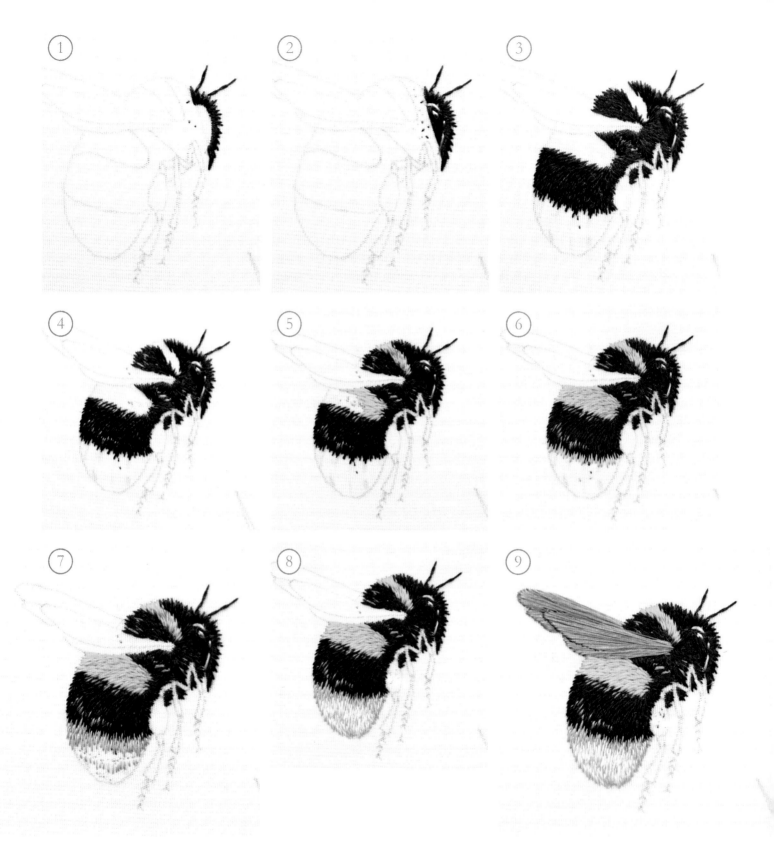

How to stitch

STEP 1: Using black (Black), sew different lengths of stitches spreading out from around the eye, and split stitch the antennae.

STEP 2: Sew the eye in black (Black) using satin stitch. Add three to four stitches of white (White) around the eye to add definition and one or two stitches within the eye to add shine – you will need to cross over the black stitches to avoid the floss sinking and getting lost.

STEP 3: The body of the bumblebee is sewn using small black stitches and following the stitch-direction guide. To make the bee appear hairy rather than sleek I haven't split the stitches, I have slipped the floss in between the previous threads. Don't be too neat around the edges of the bumblebee's body; allow your stitches to finish at different points over the template line.

STEP 4: Add a few stitches in grey (Grey) within the black to add texture to the hair.

STEP 5: Using dark yellow (Kingcup), add the first shade within the bee's stripes. As with the black, you will need to slip the stitches in between the previous threads to create the appearance of hair.

STEP 6: Complete the stripes in light yellow (Light Gold) and add a row of stitches to the bottom section of the bee.

STEP 7: Using beige (Pale Mushroom), stitch the next couple of layers in the bottom section of the bumblebee and add a few stitches in a row further down.

STEP 8: Complete the bottom of the bumblebee in cream (Mid Ecru). Again, don't be too neat finishing your stitches around the template line – allow them to vary in length.

STEP 9: Working from the furthest to the nearest wing, sew long stitches in grey (Grey). Some stitches will need to be shorter than others to allow them to overlap and not become clumped at the point. Add some stitches of light brown (Pine) to add definition.

STEP 10: The legs are sewn using long stitches in dark brown (Brown) and black (Black). I have only used one or two stitches of black on the side of the leg that would be in shadow. The small 'v'-shaped sections are stitched using one black stitch and one brown.

STEP 11: To create the pollen sac on the bumblebee's leg, fill the area with small French knots in orange (Marigold). I wound the thread around the needle twice to keep the knots small.

STEP 12: Use dark brown (Brown) for the darker side of the branch and light brown (Pine) for the lighter side. Split stitch up and down the branch, coming to a point at each end. Stitch the thorns in dark brown and light brown split stitch, sewing the length of the thorn before stitching the attaching section at an acute angle.

STEP 13: Using white (White), split stitch the outline of the flower petals, then sew the first layer of shading in long-and-short stitch.

STEP 14: Stitch the next layer of shading in blue-grey (Lavender), leaving a small space in the centre of the flower to avoid the stitching becoming too tightly packed.

STEP 15: Sew two long stitches in medium green (Forest Green) to separate each petal, meeting at a central point.

STEP 16: Add small French knots in light yellow (Light Gold) randomly around the centre of the blossom.

STEP 17: Using beige (Pale Mushroom), sew stitches stretching from the centre of the blossom to each French knot.

STEP 18: The stems and sepals of the blossoms, along with the small leaves around the flowers, should be stitched in dark green (Mermaid) and medium green (Forest Green).

STEP 19: Split stitch around the outline of the sloes in black (Black) and, following the stitch-direction lines, add a small area of long-and-short stitch to the darkest side of each berry.

STEP 20: Shade the next layer of the berry in dark blue-purple (Viola) following the direction lines.

STEP 21: Finish the berries with a layer of light blue-purple (Medium Pansy) and white (White) to add shine. Using dark green (Mermaid), outline the leaves in split stitch and, following the veins as your direction lines and the shading guide, fill with long-and-short stitch in dark green (Mermaid), medium green (Forest Green) and light green (Fir Green).

Gooseberry and Common Wasp

Ribes uva-crispa and *Vespula vulgaris*

GOOSEBERRY

There is some debate as to whether currant bushes such as the gooseberry, redcurrant and blackcurrant are native to Britain, however, there are no records of plants being introduced for cultivation or of any sort of domestic cultivation before the sixteenth century. Gooseberries and other such currants can be found growing in undisturbed, ancient habitats and it is difficult to believe that all these plants have spilled over from garden varieties. It is believed that gardeners started cultivating gooseberries from wild plants and it soon became a popular fruit to show at village competitions. By the end of the nineteenth century there were as many as 2,000 named varieties.

Sometimes called 'goosegog', this densely branched spiny shrub can be found growing in deciduous woodland, scrub, hedgerows, stream sides and sometimes under old walls on waste ground. The berries can be greenish-yellow or purplish-red with bristly hairs, they measure 10–20mm (½–¾in) and appear in late spring, usually ripening by midsummer. Gooseberries can be rather sharp in taste and are best cooked as part of a dessert such as gooseberry pie or gooseberry fool. If they are especially sharp, they can be made into jelly or jam.

It was once a popular belief that a stye could be cured by lancing with a gooseberry prickle first passed through a wedding ring. In Ireland, the thorn was just pointed at the stye with the words 'Away, away, away!'.

The shape of the gooseberry flower seems to prove particularly attractive to social wasps. Perhaps its shallow structure suits the wasp's rather short tongue, as it can often be seen feeding from the flower and aiding pollination.

COMMON WASP

Asking people to love wasps is difficult; I would be lying if I said I had never cursed their little black and yellow bodies as they dive bombed my picnic in late summer. But, contrary to popular belief, wasps do have a purpose and are truly fascinating creatures. There are over 9,000 species of wasp in the UK alone, many of which are completely harmless to humans, including parasitic wasps, some of which are so small they can only be seen under a microscope. There are around 260 species of solitary wasp and only nine species of social wasp (wasps that live within a social group).

The most frequently seen social wasps are the common and German wasp, often called jaspers, sow-waps, vespas or yellow jackets amongst other names. It can be very difficult to differentiate between the two.

An adult worker wasp will set about finding protein in the form of insects to feed to the developing larvae, killing a multitude of garden pests such as aphids and caterpillars. The adult worker will feed on a droplet of sugary liquid produced by the larvae, but they will also seek out nectar from flowers to sustain them. It is in doing this that wasps serve as important pollinators. It is mainly later in the summer, when there are fewer larvae in the nest giving out sugary treats that the wasps turn their attention to us in search of carbohydrates and sugars.

A wasp nest is a thing of beauty, created from pulped wood that has been chewed and mixed with saliva by the queen; the wasps create a spherical, paper-like structure filled with hexagonal paper cells each containing an egg. Each nest can contain 5,000–10,000 individuals. The colony will only last one year and after the new queen has departed all the other wasps will die once the weather turns cold.

It may be a stretch to ask people to love the wasp, but if not *love* then perhaps we can learn to respect it for the balance it brings to our eco-system.

Threads used

I have used Pipers Silks floss silks for this project

FOR THE WASP

Black – Pipers 'Black'
White – Pipers 'White'
Dark grey – Pipers 'Deep Slate'
Grey – Pipers 'Grey'
Dark yellow – Pipers 'Kingcup'
Medium yellow – Pipers 'Jasmine'
Light yellow – Pipers 'Citrus'
Brown – Pipers 'Brown'
Medium gold-brown – Pipers 'Antique Gold'
Light gold-brown – Pipers 'Autumn Gold'
Light beige – Pipers 'Pale Mushroom'

FOR THE GOOSEBERRY AND FRAME

Black – Pipers 'Black'
White – Pipers 'White'
Brown – Pipers 'Brown'
Medium gold-brown – Pipers 'Antique Gold'
Bright green – Pipers 'New Lettuce'
Citrus green-yellow – Pipers 'Lime Yellow'
Pink-brown – Pipers 'Rhubarb'
Dark green – Pipers 'Forest Green'
Green – Pipers 'Green'
Medium green – Pipers 'Leaf'
Light green – Pipers 'Pale Leaf'

Template: page 143

Stitches used

Long-and-short stitch (page 32)
Split stitch (page 37)

Shading guide

Stitch-direction guide

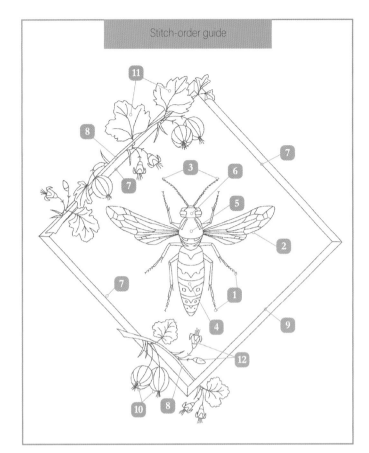

Stitch-order guide

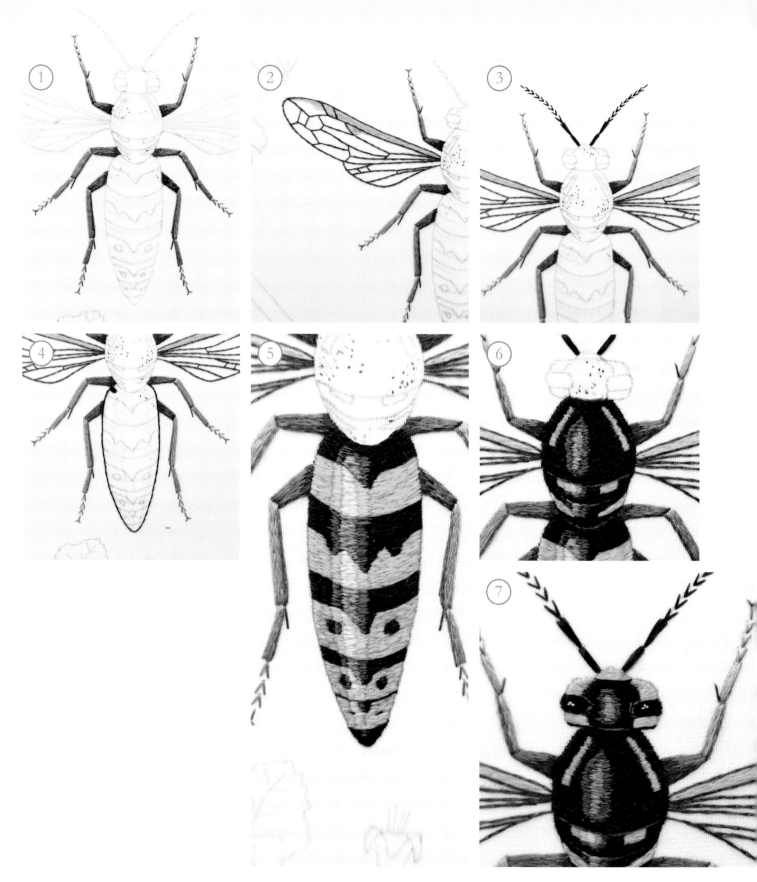

How to stitch

STEP 1: Stitch the legs of the wasp using split stitch and long-and-short stitch shading with very small 'V'-shaped stitches for the lower parts. Follow the shading guide using brown (Brown), medium gold-brown (Antique Gold) and light gold-brown (Autumn Gold).

STEP 2: To stitch the wings, start by adding a small area of shading in light beige (Pale Mushroom) to the top of each wing. Over-sew the veins in split stitch using brown (Brown).

STEP 3: Stitch the antennae in black (Black). Use long stitches for the first two sections, followed by small 'V'-shaped stitches. Finish each antenna with a single stitch. You will need to secure your thread through the stitches on the reverse.

STEP 4: Starting with the wasp's abdomen, outline in black (Black) and start to shade horizontally in long-and-short stitch following the stitch guidelines. It may help to add vertical shading guidelines to know where the light will hit.

STEP 5: Shade the abdomen using black (Black), dark grey (Deep Slate) and grey (Grey) for the dark stripes, and dark yellow (Kingcup), medium yellow (Jasmine) and light yellow (Citrus) for the light stripes. The stitches can get very small here so you may need to keep your thimble handy.

STEP 6: Following the same techniques and using the same colours as the abdomen, stitch the thorax. Add some dark grey (Deep Slate) in between each section to add definition.

STEP 7: Stitch the head using the same colours as the body and following the same light direction. The eyes are stitched in black (Black) satin stitch after the main section of the head. Add a few tiny white (White) stitches to add highlights to the eyes and add some dark grey (Deep Slate) around each eye to give it some definition.

STEP 8: Using black (Black), split stitch the first three sides of the border, as shown in the order guide.

STEP 9: Using brown (Brown) and medium gold-brown (Antique Gold), split stitch the branches and spikes. Remember that the light is coming from above so the brown will be on the underside. After the lower branch has been stitched you can finish the last border section in black.

STEP 10: The gooseberries are filled using a few stitches of pink-brown (Rhubarb) to add blush at the top and bottom where it can be seen. Then, following the vein lines for direction, fill with bright green (New Lettuce), citrus green-yellow (Lime Yellow) and white (White) highlights. Add the vein lines in citrus green-yellow, the stems in dark green (Forest Green) and four to five stitches in brown at the base of each berry. Remember to stitch the berries in the background before those in the foreground.

STEP 11: Both sides of each leaf are stitched light on the outer edge grading to dark in the centre, however, one side will use darker shades than the other. Following the shading guide and the veins for direction, stitch the lighter side in light green (Pale Leaf), medium green (Leaf) and green (Green). The darker side uses medium green (Leaf), green (Green) and dark green (Forest Green). The veins are stitched in light green (Pale Leaf).

STEP 12: Finally, the buds and flowers are sewn using dark green (Forest Green), green (Green) and medium green (Leaf) with pink-brown (Rhubarb) for the petals and brown (Brown) stitches coming from the centre.

my previous work

Bee on lavender ›

4 x 5cm (1½ x 2in); silk floss on silk dupion

This was my first framed insect embroidery and was inspired by a photograph taken in my back garden in 2012. I had one lavender bush and I was fascinated by how many bees were attracted to it, so I got my camera and patiently took shot after blurry shot. Finally, I got one bee that stayed still long enough for me take a decent photograph and that was it, I was hooked. Since then my family have had to get used to waiting for me on walks as I snap interesting bugs with dreams of creating insect-inspired embroideries. I now have about eight lavender bushes in my garden and intend to get many more.

‹ Wasp sipping nectar

9 x 8.5cm (3½ x 3¼in); silk floss on silk-cotton

I took this photo in my parent's garden, which is a beautiful combination of neatly presented flower beds and gentle wilderness. The hedges are a mix of standard hedging plants, blackberries and any other plant that has mingled in. It was in one of these hedges that I spotted many wasps drinking from the variety of flowers hidden within the branches, they weren't worried by my presence and left me alone to take a few shots. People often think that wasps aren't pollinators as they aren't hairy like bees, but in this shot the tiny hairs on a wasp's body are clearly visible. Stitching the hairs proved to be difficult – silk thread just wasn't fine enough – then someone suggested I try hair. So, stitching with thread from my own head, I gave this little wasp the hairs that prove why they are such important pollinators.

Wood ant ˇ

5.5 x 2.5cm (2¼ x 1in); silk floss on silk dupion

I had just bought some macro filters for my camera when I took this photo in Wentwood forest, South Wales. Wood ants are fascinating creatures – they build large nests on the woodland floor and perform several important roles in the forest eco-system, from improving soil in the excavation of their nests to feeding many of the other woodland creatures. If a nest is disturbed, wood ants will spray formic acid in defense and some birds will utilize this to repel lice and mites. They will also distribute the seeds of certain plants such as violets and some rare flowers such as small cow-wheat. So if you are lucky enough to find a wood-ant nest take a closer look, but try not to disturb the ants.

ˆ Garden spider

6 x 4cm (2½ x 1½in); silk floss on silk dupion

One of my favourite sights in autumn is all the spider webs that decorate the garden, stretching from plant to plant and glistening with dew in the morning. It was one of those webs that I tried to photograph back in 2014. I had never really looked at the markings on a garden spider before, but I was amazed at the intricate patterns on its abdomen, which seemed to fit perfectly with embroidery and stitch direction. I am normally scared of spiders, but spending several weeks stitching this one certainly improved my relationship with the garden variety. It was this piece that made me realize that we shouldn't always focus on the traditionally pretty, popular insects – they are all fascinating and deserving of art.

Comb-footed spider on a rose ›

6.5 x 5cm (2½ x 2in); silk floss on cotton fabric, dyed with wild strawberry leaves

The green of this spider shone out against the red rose in my front garden; the beautiful contrast of colours was too good not to stitch. Often found in hedgerows, grasslands and gardens from late spring to mid-autumn, the comb-footed spider will feed on flies and other insects. I like to think that this spider was guarding the rose and protecting it from aphids, like a tiny gardener. The legs of this spider are rather translucent and that proved to be a challenge when stitching – I have mixed some of the red thread with the green to create the effect.

Mother Shipton moth ›

4 x 3cm (1½ x 1¼in); silk floss on silk-cotton

Wouldn't it be wonderful to be immortalized in a moth's wing?
The Mother Shipton moth gets its name from the pattern on its
wings, which is said to resemble a witch's face. Ursula Southall was
born in 1488, and was a renowned fortune teller known as Mother
Shipton. Her unusual appearance fuelled witchcraft rumours and
she became Yorkshire's most famous witch and prophetess. Many
of her predictions are now known to have been written in 1871
by a man named Hindley but her fame still lives on. Her cave still
remains as a memorial and is a well-known tourist attraction, and
the image of a witch on a moth's wing is still said to be Mother
Shipton. Oh, to live on in a moth's wing!

‹ Lords-and-ladies

17 x 6.5cm (7 x 2½in); silk floss on silk-cotton

This was another photograph taken on the walk to school.
I had seen many lords-and-ladies but this was the most perfect
specimen with the morning sun shining on it. I used a little
artistic licence putting the red berries alongside the flower as they
would not normally appear until the autumn months, but I felt
I would be telling only half the story to show just the flower.
The spider was also part of the piece's story; as I often sew in
my summerhouse I frequently get little guests, and one morning
a running spider was sitting on the embroidery. I took a
photograph of it and posted it on social media... people thought
it was part of the work, so I added it.

Magpie moth ›

9.5 x 6.5cm (4 x 2½in); silk floss on silk dupion, dyed using black elder leaves

I spotted this magpie moth on a brick wall in my garden back in 2017. It was the first time I had ever seen one and I was fascinated – it certainly counters the idea that all moths are dull brown creatures. The caterpillars have similar colouration to the adult and feed on plants such as blackthorn, hawthorn and gooseberry bushes while the adult moth feeds on nectar and is an excellent pollinator. This piece took about 64 hours to sew.

‹ Frog and woodlouse

12 x 10cm (4¾ x 4in); silk floss on silk-cotton

This is my most ambitious work to date and took over six months of stitching. I wasn't sure whether it would be too complicated but the photograph kept drawing me back. I had spotted the frog on the side of our garden pond and wanted to take a picture for reference purposes, but it wasn't until afterwards that I spotted the tiny woodlouse bending up towards the frog as if in conversation with it. Some people think that the woodlouse is scared of the frog, but I preferred a different narrative. I once read an article suggesting that one calm woodlouse can soothe more anxious woodlice within the group, demonstrating a wonderful example of social interaction and creating stability. So, I made this my guru woodlouse, sitting on his bed of colourful petals surrounded by calming chamomile, counselling the anxious frog.

Large copper butterfly ›

7 x 5cm (2¾ x 2in); silk floss on silk-cotton

Cardiff museum has a wonderful Natural History department that very kindly allowed me to photograph some of their insect collection with a focus on endangered and extinct species in the UK. One insect of interest to me was the large copper butterfly. While it can still be found in small colonies in Europe, it has been extinct in the UK for over 150 years. Once common in East Anglia, its demise was the result of changing fenland management and the draining of the fens. There have been several attempts to reintroduce the species but unfortunately all have failed and it remains extinct in the UK.

˄ Cicada

13 x 6cm (5 x 2½in); silk floss on silk/cotton

This is another insect photographed at Cardiff museum. While not completely extinct in the UK, they are classed as endangered as the only known cicadas are found in the New Forest on the south coast of England. Even then the last known sighting was in the early 1990s. Threats to the New Forest cicada include loss of habitat and the plants on which they lay their eggs, plus climate change, with wetter weather becoming more frequent. When I photographed the cicada I was fascinated by its translucent wings; I tried to re-create this by using florist's cellophane stitched onto the fabric then trimming around the stitching.

‹ Banded snail

5 x 8cm (2 x 3¼in); silk floss on silk-cotton

Also known as a brown or white-lipped snail, these beautiful visitors are common in many gardens. The colour and pattern of different snails can vary greatly from light to dark and they can have up to five bands or none at all. Stitching the curves on the shell proved to be tricky but the shading on the leaf was a joy. I understand that snails are not always a gardener's friend but they

can play an important role in decomposition and are a vital food source for much of our wildlife. Gardeners will often put down pellets to kill slugs and snails, but this can be harmful to wildlife such as hedgehogs once it has entered the food chain, so it is best to try other methods if possible.

‹ Seven-spot ladybird

5 x 5cm (2 x 2in); silk floss on silk-cotton

This embroidery is very close to my heart as it won me 'Needlecrafter of the Year 2018' at the Knitting and Stitching show in London, UK. Unfortunately, I couldn't make it to accept my award as a terrible snowstorm meant I couldn't leave Wales, but the pride I felt on hearing that I had won made me dance around the kitchen. The embroidery took a relatively short amount of time compared to my other pieces, roughly three weeks, but it was this win that fuelled my belief that the beauty and simplicity of a single insect is something that everyone can appreciate.

Wasp beetle ›

Silk floss on silk-cotton fabric; framed in a 15.25cm (6in) embroidery hoop

I have only ever seen a wasp beetle once and I unfortunately didn't manage to get a photograph. My daughter and I were walking to school and found it on the pavement in the path of many trampling feet, and as our priority was to move it out of harm's way, I didn't manage a picture. But I was so inspired by its beautiful markings that this example was created using other source material. The wasp beetle is classified as a longhorn beetle; the larvae live in dead wood and the adults can be seen from late spring into summer feeding on pollen from hedgerow flowers, gardens and the edge of woodlands. While their markings may mimic that of a wasp for protection, they are completely harmless and excellent pollinators.

templates

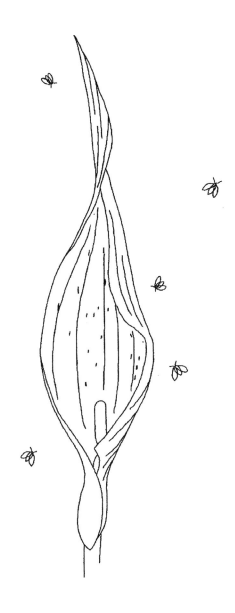

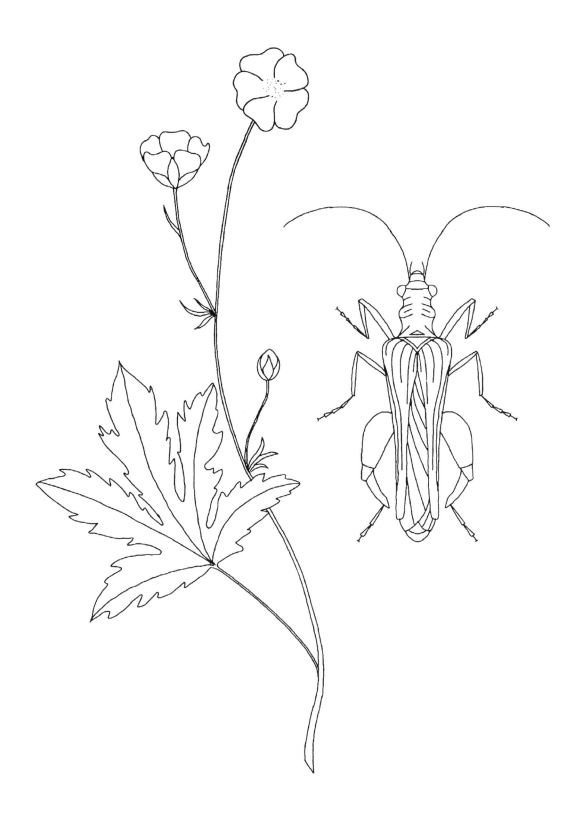

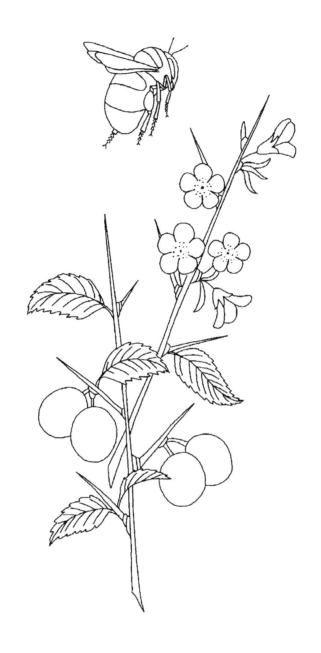

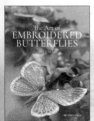
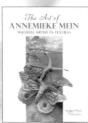

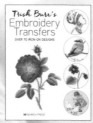

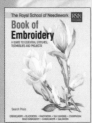